D0185800

TEXTS FROM DOG

First published in 2012
by HEADLINE PUBLISHING GROUP

2

Cataloguing in Publication Data is available from the British Library

Hardback ISBN 978 1 4722 0070 9

Printed and bound in Italy by Rotolito Lombarda S.p.A.

Headline's policy is to use papers that are natural, renewable and recyclable products and made from
wood grown in sustainable forests. The logging and manufacturing processes are expected to conform
to the environmental regulations of the country of origin.

HEADLINE PUBLISHING GROUP
An Hachette UK Company
338 Euston Road
London NW1 3BH

www.headline.co.uk
www.hachette.co.uk

headline

INTRODOGTION

HELLO.

My name is Dog, and this book is pretty much all about me.
For boozillions (is that a number?) of years, you humans have been obsessed with dogs. You love us, and we pretend to love you, because you have biscuits and you stroke our bellies like idiots.
We're like BFFs. Best Friends FOREVER.
Now, when human geeks invented the internet in 1811 (I think) it gave you a way to appreciate your Dogs on a WHOLE NEW LEVEL.
Oh yes.
Dogs on skateboards. Dogs on surfboards. Singing Dogs. Dancing Dogs. Dogs wearing glasses. Dogs wearing PANTS.
You guys just can't get enough of us...

...Well, guess what.
I'm a Digital Dog in a Digital Age, and I'm pushing the Human/Dog relationship further than it's ever gone before.
How?
I learned a new trick. Yes siree.
I have a phone, and I'm not afraid to use it.
The following pages are a testament to Dogular intelligence.
A collection of text messages sent from me to my idiot human.
This is the first stage. The next step is canine world domination.

WOOF.

18:16
Messages
Dog
Edit
I'VE GOT UNLIMITED TEXTS
I'VE GOT UNLIMITED TEXTS
I'VE GOT UNLIMITED TEXTS
I'VE GOT UNLIMITED TEXTS
I'VE GOT UNLIMITED TEXTS
I'VE GOT UNLIMITED TEXTS
Oh God. This is horrible
Text Message
Send

18:18
Messages
Dog
Edit
WOOF
Yes?
DID YOU GET THAT TEXT?
Yes
THE WOOF ONE?
YES
OMFG THIS IS AWESOME
Yeah
Text Message
Send

12:30
Messages
Dog
Edit
Fun day. Ran around the house in a cape. I'M BATDOG LOL
Where did you get the cape?
I think role playing helps alleviate my boredom. I feel so alive x
WHERE DID YOU GET THE CAPE?
I PULLED THE CURTAIN RAIL DOWN. JESUS. WHY CAN'T YOU JUST BE HAPPY FOR ME?
Text Message
Send

12:16
Messages
Dog
Edit
So you throw the stick
Yep
I fetch it, and bring it back
Correct
Then what?
I throw it again
What for?
So you can bring it back
SO WHAT THE HELL IS MY MOTIVATION?
Text Message
Send

12:24
Messages
Dog
Edit
WHERE IS MR DUCK?
Oh, he's around
Let's make a deal
WHERE IS MR DUCK?
You can have Mr Duck back, if you stop pissing on my bed
LET ME SPEAK TO MR DUCK
QUACK
ARE YOU OK MR DUCK?
He's fine. FOR NOW
Text Message
Send

13:10
Messages
Dog
Edit
I want a pet
You are a pet
Can't pets have pets?
What if THAT pet wants a pet?
A pet's pet's pet?
I'm terminating this conversation
Text Message
Send

06:31
Messages
Dog
Edit
You bought dog shampoo
Yes
Are you going to try and give me a bath?
I WILL give you a bath
DEATH. FIRST.
Text Message
Send

12:13
Messages
Dog
Edit
I need latex for my BATDOG costume
No
DUDE, this is important. I need to look sexy when I'm fighting crime
Stop being weird
What's weird about a dog in latex with rubber nipples?
WHY DO YOU NEED RUBBER NIPPLES?
OMG. FOR ADDED SEXINESS. DUMBASS
Text Message
Send

18:52
Messages
Dog
Edit
I'M A TEXTING DOG
Yep
WHERE DO I KEEP MY PHONE?
I don't know
DOGS DON'T HAVE POCKETS
SSHHHHHHH
I FIND THIS WHOLE THING VERY SUSPICIOUS
Text Message
Send

20:44
Messages
Dog
Edit
If I shag one of the Queen's Corgis would that make me royalty?
No
What if I shagged the Queen's leg?
That would make you a Duke
Dude, we HAVE to go to London
Text Message
Send

18:03
Messages
Dog
Edit
BEEN THINKING ABOUT REINCARNATION
Deep
IN OUR NEXT LIFE, YOU BE THE DOG, I'LL BE THE OWNER
Sure. You can go to work, make the money and pay the bills
NEW PLAN: WE'LL BOTH BE DOGS. BUT I'LL GET MORE GIRLS
Text Message
Send

13:18
Messages
Dog
Edit
BEEN CHASING MY TAIL FOR 45 MINUTES
Productive
WHAT HAPPENS IF I CATCH IT?
The universe implodes
AWESOME
Text Message
Send

18:30
Messages
Dog
Edit
CATCAT is in the garden
Who's CATCAT?
I'm BATDOG. Half Dog. Half Bat
Ok
CATCAT is a super villain. Half Cat. Half Cat
So... a cat
Basically. But EVIL
Basically, a cat
Are you not taking this threat seriously?
Text Message
Send

21:35
Messages
Dog
Edit
Have you got crisps upstairs?
No
I thought I heard a bag rustling
You were mistaken
I'll come up and check
FFS alright I HAVE got crisps but they're MINE
Yeah
I'll just come up and watch you eat them
Text Message
Send

18:44
Messages
Dog
Edit
I'M DRUNK
HOW?
ME AND TED THE TERRIER WENT TO A BAR
THEY DIDN'T NOTICE WE WERE TWO DOGS IN A TRENCHCOAT
Oh my God
I LOVE YOU SO MUCH
Text Message
Send

12:58
Messages
Dog
Edit
Almost got our trophy this morning
Our trophy?
Remember?
Remember what?
You said 'I'd really like the Postman's finger on the mantelpiece'
THAT DOESN'T SOUND LIKE SOMETHING I'D SAY
LOL You're silly x
YOU'RE INSANE
Text Message
Send

11:29
Messages
Dog
Edit
If you buy me sausages EVERY day for the next 6 weeks I'll teach you how to speak dog
DEAL
We'll start with the basics: 'WOOF'
Right, what does 'WOOF' mean?
EVERYTHING. NOW BUY ME SAUSAGES
YOU SNEAKY FAT TWAT BADGER
Text Message
Send

09:56
Messages
Dog
Edit
Are you calling me?
Did you POO in my HAT?
Yep
Christ. Dogs are assholes. You just do what you WANT. You don't think of the CONSEQUENCES
Yeah. OMG. Remember when that DOG invented the ATOMIC BOMB?
Forget it
Was Hitler a chihuahua?
Text Message
Send

06:21
Messages
Dog
Edit
I BELIEVE I CAN FLY
I BELIEVE I CAN TOUCH THE SKY
I'M ON MY FIRST TEST FLIGHT TODAY
I MADE SOME WINGS OUT OF YOUR DUVET
Oh God
Text Message
Send

Pork Bits

07:07
Messages
Dog
Edit
STILL HUNGRY
You've had breakfast
WANT MORE BREAKFAST
You'll get fat
WHAT'S 'FAT'?
It's what happens when you eat too much food
FAT SOUNDS AWESOME. LET'S GET FAT
Text Message
Send

08:30
Messages
Dog
Edit
BEEN PLAYING WITH MY RUBBER BONER
Bone
Oh
What's a boner?
Something TOTALLY different
Text Message
Send

19:25
Messages
Dog
Edit
Watching Ocean's Eleven
Stop touching my DVDs
Dude, Brad Pitt is one handsome human
Yep
He makes you look like a baboon's ass
Text Message
Send

12:03
Messages
Dog
Edit
I JUST SAW A SKATEBOARDING BULLDOG ON YOUTUBE
You're not getting a skateboard
WELL DUH. WE NEED TO GO BIGGER
You're not getting a motorbike
I NEED A MONKEY COSTUME AND A SPEEDBOAT
Text Message
Send

14:21
Messages
Dog
Edit
Just woke up
It's almost 3pm
What's 3pm?
The time
What's 'time'?
Seriously?
Will it take long to explain? I need to lie down
Text Message
Send

20:54
Messages
Dog
Edit
JUST HAD TO GO BATDOG ON A DUCK'S ASS
What does that even mean?
WHO CARES? IT SOUNDS GANGSTA
Text Message
Send

23:08
Messages
Dog
Edit
SUPER FUN DAY
What did you do?
SAME THING I DO EVERY DAY
I'M A DOG
EVERY DAY IS SUPER FUN DAY
I hate you
Text Message
Send

22:28
Messages
Dog
Edit
Fetch the stick
No
Fetch the stick
No
Fetch the stick
No
Fetch the stick
NO
FETCH THE STICK
BUY A BOOMERANG DIPSHIT
Text Message
Send

16:30
Messages
Dog
Edit
HOW COME YOU GOT NO GIRLFRIEND?
It's complicated
WANT SOME SEX TIPS?
Not from you
TIP NUMBER 1:
NO THANK YOU
SEXY BUM SNIFFING...
Text Message
Send

13:03
Messages
Dog
Edit
MY EAR IS ITCHING
Scratch it
MY EAR IS ITCHING
Scratch it
MY EAR IS ITCHING
Scratch it
MY EAR IS ITCHING
Scratch it
MY EAR IS ITCHING
Kill me
Text Message
Send

13:48
Messages
Dog
Edit
WHY ARE YOU SUCH A CLEAN FREAK?
WTF
WHY DOES EVERYTHING HAVE TO BE SPOTLESS?
Calm down
POLISH THE GLASS POLISH THE GLASS
You ran into the patio door again
I COULD HAVE DIED YOU TWATFACED TWO-LEGGED BUMHOLE
Text Message
Send

18:53
Messages
Dog
Edit
WHERE IS MR DUCK?
Under the cupboard in the living room
DON'T PUT HIM UNDER THERE. HE GETS CLAUSTROPHOBIC
It's nice that you care about Mr Duck
I WANNA BITE HIS HEAD
Lovely
Text Message
Send

16:38
Messages
Dog
Edit
I'M LYING IN THE GARDEN
That's nice
IT IS NICE
WHAT ARE YOU DOING?
I'm busy. At work
Oh
I'M LYING IN THE GARDEN
I FUCKING KNOW
Text Message
Send

18:59
Messages
Dog
Edit
WE HAVE TO LEAVE THE COUNTRY
Why
GOT IN TROUBLE WITH SOME PEOPLE
Which people?
BAD PEOPLE
WHICH PEOPLE?
SQUIRREL MAFIA
Text Message
Send

18:40
Messages
Dog
Edit
Sister-in-law just called. Nephew left Lego Luke Skywalker at our house. Have you seen him?
I'm afraid he's gone over to The Dark Side
Right
Soon he'll be Poop Skywalker
Yeah ok
He's going to meet ARSE VADER
YOU SWALLOWED HIM. I GET IT
Text Message
Send

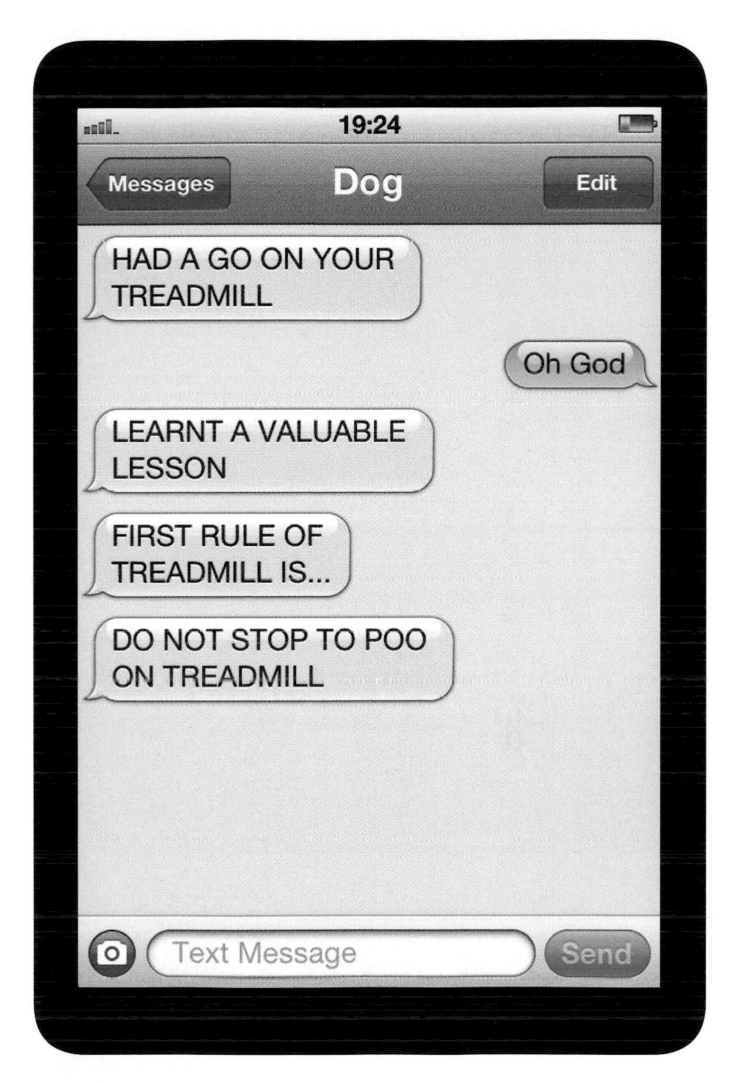
19:24
Messages
Dog
Edit
HAD A GO ON YOUR TREADMILL
Oh God
LEARNT A VALUABLE LESSON
FIRST RULE OF TREADMILL IS...
DO NOT STOP TO POO ON TREADMILL
Text Message
Send

11:14
Messages
Dog
Edit
I want a new look
Right
I want you to shave me bald
When I showed you how to text, I thought we might have profound, insightful conversations that would give us a greater understanding of our relationship
Yeah.
Shave me bald
Text Message
Send

19:00
Messages
Dog
Edit
ME AND TED THE TERRIER JUST ACCIDENTALLY LICKED EACH OTHERS TONGUES
So?
WILL TED GET PREGNANT?
Yes
OH GOD
Text Message
Send

20:52
Messages
Dog
Edit
You need to get over your fear of squirrels
Dude, I'm BATDOG
I ain't afraid of no squirrel
OMFG DON'T TELL THAT EVIL BASTARD WHERE I LIVE
Text Message
Send

12:46
Messages
Dog
Edit
Cómo estás?
WTF?
Woah. Wrong person
You speak Spanish?
Yeah. But I'm not illegally importing Spanish dog biscuits into the country, if that's what you're thinking
I wasn't thinking that
Good
I am now
Bollocks
Text Message
Send

09:51
Messages
Dog
Edit
JUST BURNED MY NOSE ON THE HEATER
Don't put your nose on the heater
Right
JUST BURNED MY NOSE ON THE HEATER
DON'T PUT YOUR NOSE ON THE HEATER
Ah. Gotcha
JUST BURNED MY NOSE ON THE HEATER
DO IT AGAIN
Text Message
Send

15:52
Messages
Dog
Edit
We should probably move house
Why?
The neighbours hate us
WHY
Don't get mad...
I accidentally dick-slapped their cat
Text Message
Send

07:23
Messages
Dog
Edit
Namuh!
What does that mean?
That's 'human' spelt backwards
Hey, what's DOG spelt backwards?
OMG
Yeah. Sorry for BLOWING YOUR MIND
Text Message
Send

21:10
Messages
Dog
Edit
I have a question about 'Time'
Is it a stupid question?
No DOUCHEBAG
It's a SMART question
Fire away
DO YEARS HAVE EARS?
Text Message
Send

13:32
Messages
Dog
Edit
KNOCKED BIN OVER. DRANK SOME STUFF
What stuff?
DUNNO. BLUE SILVER STUFF. ANGRY COW
Red Bull?
PROBABLY. BRAIN FEELS ALL ELECTRICKY
Lie down
BEEN BURYING STUFF
WHAT STUFF?
MICROWAVE N SHIT
Text Message
Send

11:01
Messages
Dog
Edit
SWALLOWED YOUR USB STICK ON PURPOSE
WHY WOULD YOU DO THAT?
I AM NOW PART DOG, PART MACHINE
BATDOG IS BIONIC
You'll poo it out
I'LL NEVER POO AGAIN
Text Message
Send

12:08
Messages
Dog
Edit
Had a nice chat with a policeman
A policeman?
Yeah. I was like 'Woof! Woof officer!' LOL
Ok
He was like 'TAKE YOUR PAWS OFF THE STEERING WHEEL AND GET OUT OF THE CAR'
OMFG
What's a 'lawyer'? He says you need one
Text Message
Send

12:33
Messages
Dog
Edit
Use the word 'literally' in a sentence
You are LITERALLY the most annoying dog in the world
So, literally means 'the opposite of'
Yes. You are literally the stupidest life form in the known universe
LOL, I'm not THAT smart x
Text Message
Send

18:58
Messages
Dog
Edit
How come my hair never grows longer than an inch?
I shave you while you sleep
When you're asleep I fart on your head
I'M JOKING
Oh
I'm not
Text Message
Send

20:23
Messages
Dog
Edit
Am I a pedigree dog?
Yes
Excellent
If you want, I'll let you kiss my paw
Text Message
Send

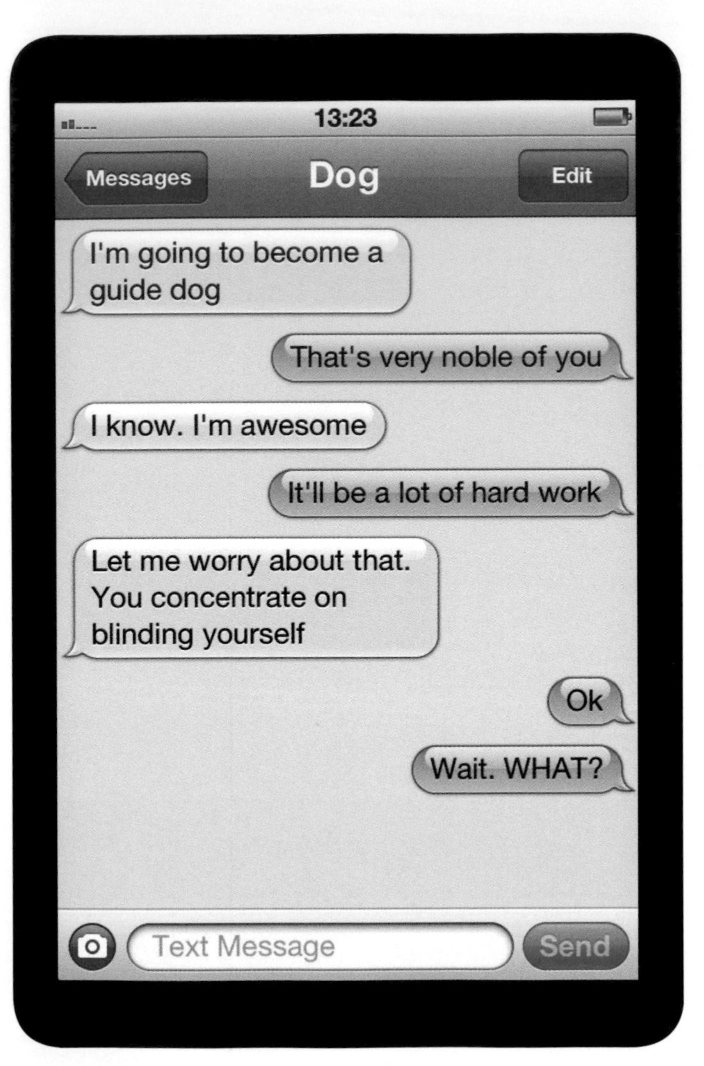
13:23
Messages
Dog
Edit
I'm going to become a guide dog
That's very noble of you
I know. I'm awesome
It'll be a lot of hard work
Let me worry about that. You concentrate on blinding yourself
Ok
Wait. WHAT?
Text Message
Send

10:44
Messages
Dog
Edit
I AM BATDOG THE UNSTOPPABLE
I think you're exaggerating
I THINK YOU'RE FRIGHTENED OF MY RAW CANINE POWER
I don't think you're 'unstoppable'
THAT'S WHAT THE PATIO DOOR THOUGHT. WENT RIGHT THROUGH THAT BITCH
HOLY SHIT
I FEEL SUPER SEXY
Text Message
Send

12:33
Messages
Dog
Edit
Just washed the dishes
How?
You're welcome
HOW?
Most dogs wouldn't have bothered
HOW DID YOU WASH THEM?
WITH MY TONGUE YOU UNGRATEFUL BITCH. JEEZ
Text Message
Send

08:17
Messages
Dog
Edit
Are you in church?
I'm in bed
I'M TELLING JESUS
Text Message
Send

13:57
Messages
Dog
Edit
Me and CATCAT did BATTLE in the garden
Ok
It was a CLASH OF THE TITANS
Right
AN ALL OUT WAR
Who won?
THERE ARE NO REAL VICTORS IN WAR
Got your ass kicked?
Little bit
Text Message
Send

19:02
Messages
Dog
Edit
OMG NEW POSTMAN
LEAVE HIM ALONE
YOU KNOW I CAN'T
LEAVE. HIM. ALONE
HE DOESN'T KNOW ANY OF MY MOVES
LEAVE HIM ALONE
LISTEN MONKEY ASS. YOU DO YOUR JOB, I'LL DO MINE
Text Message
Send

08:50
Messages
Dog
Edit
Why are you keeping another dog in the bedroom?
Christ, how many times - That's a MIRROR. The dog is YOU
Oh, yeah
Why are you keeping another dog in the bedroom?
STOP GOING IN THE FUCKING BEDROOM
Text Message
Send

13:11
Messages
Dog
Edit
CATCAT HATH RETURNED!
UH-OH
What are CATCAT'S super powers?
He has ONE eye and THREE legs
Your ARCH NEMESIS is a half blind, three legged cat?
Pretty scary right?
Text Message
Send

18:57
Messages
Dog
Edit
BEEN BUSY
Doing what?
LICKING
Licking what?
EVERYTHING
THE WHOLE HOUSE IS NOW COVERED WITH A LAYER OF MY SALIVA
YOU'RE WELCOME
Text Message
Send

14:39
Messages
Dog
Edit
I told Ted the Terrier about you teaching me to text
And?
He thinks we're freaks
We're not freaks
Yeah we are
Yeah I know :(
Text Message
Send

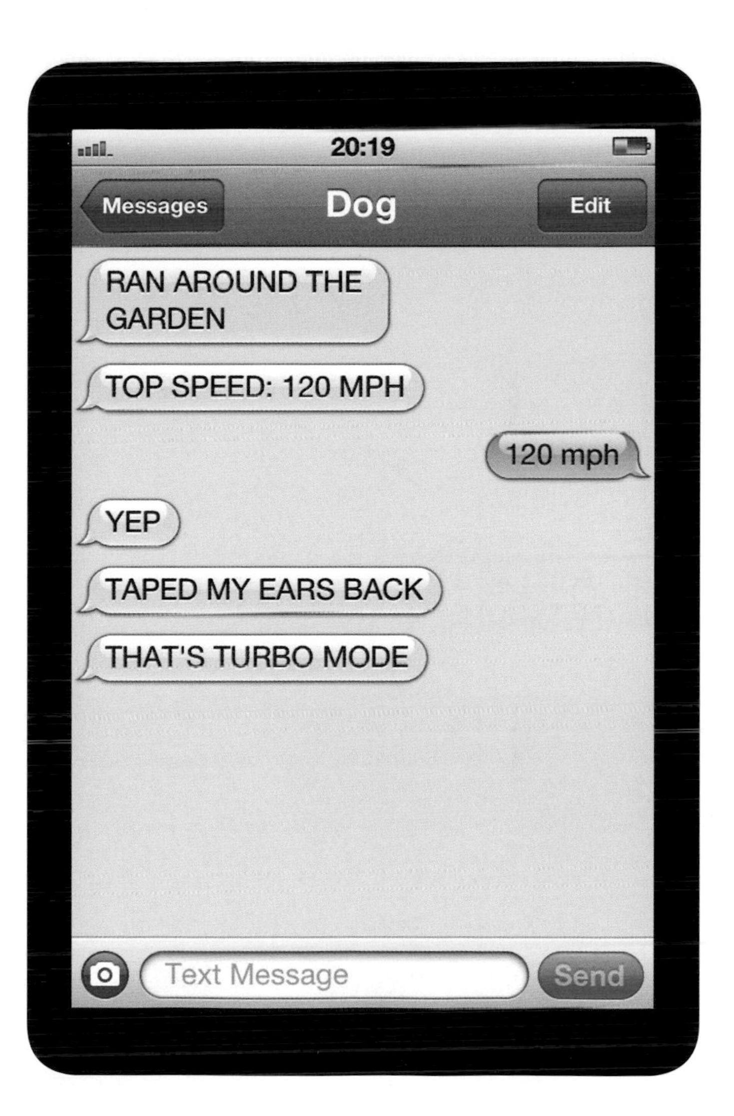
20:19
Messages
Dog
Edit
RAN AROUND THE GARDEN
TOP SPEED: 120 MPH
120 mph
YEP
TAPED MY EARS BACK
THAT'S TURBO MODE
Text Message
Send

15:02
Messages
Dog
Edit
I WANT A DIVORCE
That's not how our relationship works
I'M SICK OF YOUR SHIT
Right
I WANT MORE FROM LIFE
I've got pizza
I SUDDENLY LOVE YOU SO MUCH IT HURTS
Text Message
Send

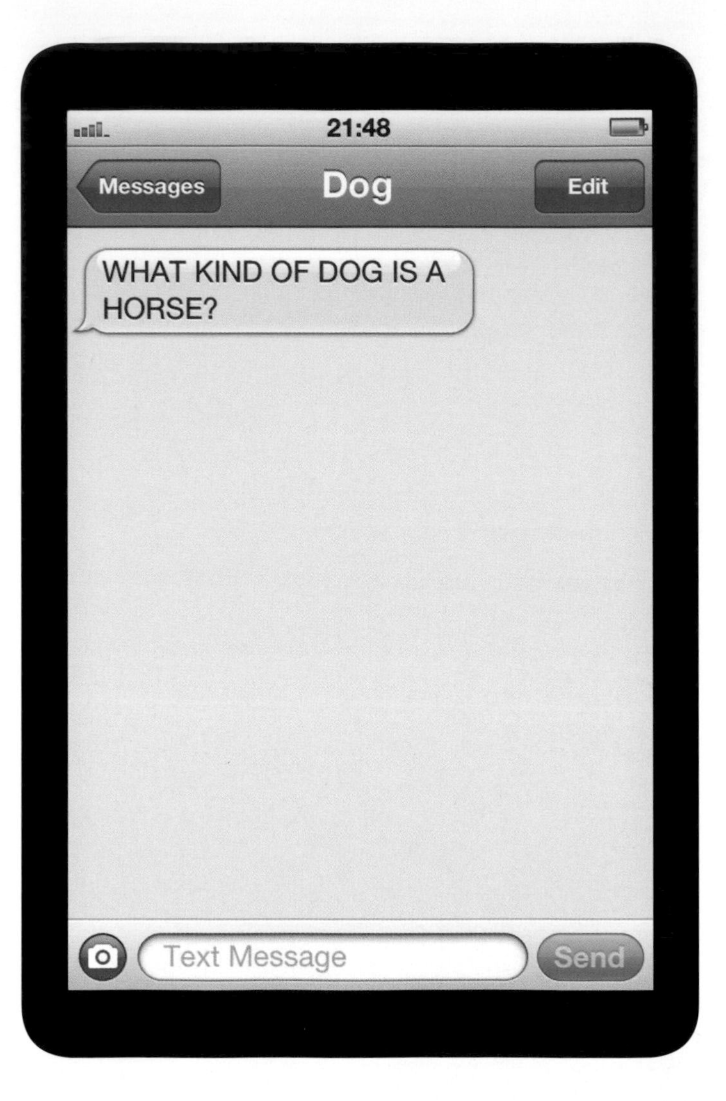
21:48
Messages
Dog
Edit
WHAT KIND OF DOG IS A HORSE?
Text Message
Send

19:08
Messages
Dog
Edit
BATDOG and CATCAT have JOINED FORCES
That's good
We TEAMED UP to knock the bin over
Now we're eating garbage
That's not good
Text Message
Send

15:10
Messages
Dog
Edit
Let's go to the park
Aw. Do you wanna play catch? Does the wittle doggy wanna play CATCH?
I want you to teach me about 'dogging'
We're never going to the park again
Text Message
Send

15:25
Messages
Dog
Edit
Do you think dogs and humans will ever be seen as equal?
I doubt it
Yeah
I guess humans are WAY too far behind
Text Message
Send

12:56
Messages
Dog
Edit
Practising karate with my new sidekick
What happened to Zombie Pigeon?
Head fell off
Who's the new guy?
Flat Squirrel
What are his special skills?
Mainly getting hit by cars
Useful
Text Message
Send

12:51
Messages
Dog
Edit
I love my new ball
Good
Did you buy me this because you feel guilty for taking me away from my mum when I was little?
I loved her so much
I'll buy you a bigger ball
SO MUCH
AND A RUBBER HAMBURGER
If you insist xx
Text Message
Send

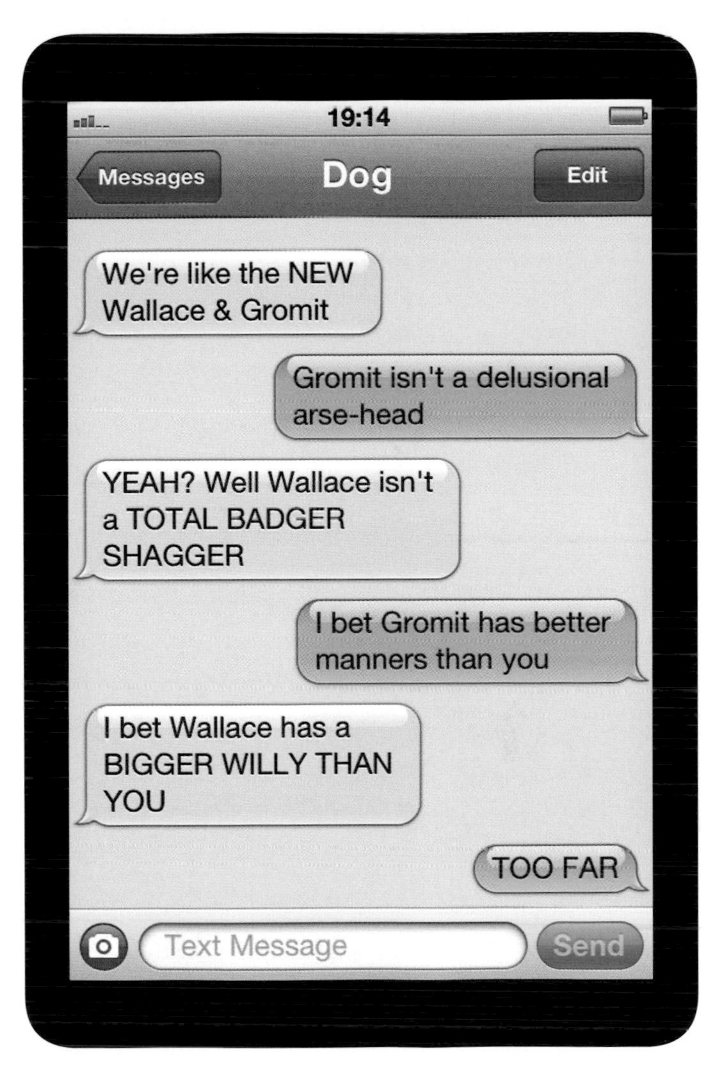
19:14
Messages
Dog
Edit
We're like the NEW Wallace & Gromit
Gromit isn't a delusional arse-head
YEAH? Well Wallace isn't a TOTAL BADGER SHAGGER
I bet Gromit has better manners than you
I bet Wallace has a BIGGER WILLY THAN YOU
TOO FAR
Text Message
Send

14:43
Messages
Dog
Edit
Why am I in the kitchen?
We have a guest who's afraid of dogs
Oh. A pansy ass
Nope. He's just a bit uncomfortable with dogs
PANSY ASS
Dude, you're scared of Henry the Hoover
DUDE, Henry the Hoover is a dust-snorting SMACK HEAD
Text Message
Send

19:40
Messages
Dog
Edit
I think I might be depressed
WHAT'S THIS?
THAT'S A BALL
OH MY GOD OH MY GOD OH MY GOD OH MY GOD OH MY GOD OH MY GOD
THIS IS THE BEST DAY OF MY ENTIRE LIFE
Text Message
Send

09:11
Messages
Dog
Edit
I want a new career
Seriously? But you've worked so hard to become CEO of Lazy Bastard Inc.
Is it difficult to become a Doctor?
It's VERY difficult for a human. For a dog - EASY
I KNEW it
You'll be doing surgery this time NEXT WEEK
SO EXCITED
Text Message
Send

15:58
Messages
Dog
Edit
Did you find the stick?
WHAT'S SO SPECIAL ABOUT THIS STICK?
Find the stick
THERE ARE MILLIONS OF STICKS IN THIS PARK
Find the stick
ARE YOU HAVING A PSYCHOLOGICAL BREAKDOWN?
Find the stick
BECAUSE I THINK I AM
Text Message
Send

13:16
Messages
Dog
Edit
I'm watching TV
Stop touching my stuff
Are the people you see on TV actually trapped inside it?
LOL. Yeah. Tiny TV people
I'll set them free
IT'S A JOKE DICKHEAD
You LIAR. It's all circuit boards and plastic
Text Message
Send

15:53
Messages
Dog
Edit
Just finished War & Peace
IMPRESSIVE
What did you think?
Tasted like chicken
Text Message
Send

08:55
Messages
Dog
Edit
I need a girlfriend
You can't have kids. I had you "fixed". Remember?
What?!
I had you "snipped"
WHAT?!
I read a book that said if you weren't planning on breeding your bulldog, you should get them neutered, because in later life they get frustrated. I did it because I love you x
FUCK YOU HITLER
Text Message
Send

14:22
Messages
Dog
Edit
Ted the Terrier's owner takes him to the park EVERY DAY
Ted's owner is unemployed
You should try and be more unemployed
Would you like to live on the street?
I'D LIKE TO LIVE IN THE PARK
Text Message
Send

13:08
Messages
Dog
Edit
I've been thinking a lot about Jesus
That's deep
When I look at Jesus, my head gets full of BIG QUESTIONS
Hmm. Like what?
WHY CAN'T DOGS GROW AWESOME BEARDS?
OMG. You could be DOG JESUS
I KNOW
Text Message
Send

06:25
Messages
Dog
Edit
INTERNET'S DOWN
Restart the router
PHONE LINE'S DOWN
That's weird
CABLE'S DOWN
WHAT'S GOING ON?
I'M TAKING EVERYTHING DOWN. JUST HIT THE TV WITH A LEG SWEEP
Text Message
Send

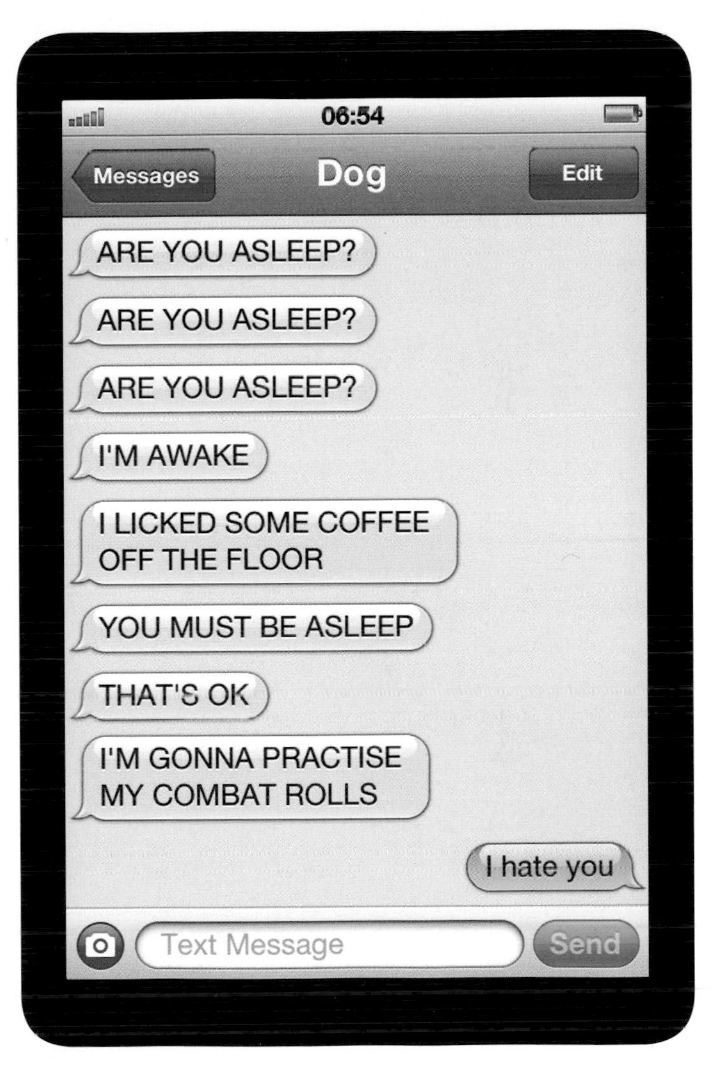
06:54
Messages
Dog
Edit
ARE YOU ASLEEP?
ARE YOU ASLEEP?
ARE YOU ASLEEP?
I'M AWAKE
I LICKED SOME COFFEE OFF THE FLOOR
YOU MUST BE ASLEEP
THAT'S OK
I'M GONNA PRACTISE MY COMBAT ROLLS
I hate you
Text Message
Send

16:07
Messages
Dog
Edit
WOOF WOOF WOOF WOOF WOOF WOOF WOOF WOOF WOOF WOOF WOOF WOOF WOOF WOOF WOOF WOOF WOOF WOOF WOOF WOOF WOOF WOOF WOOF WOOF WOOF WOOF WOOF
I could have bought a hamster
I KNOW
BUT THINK OF THE FUN YOU'D BE MISSING
Text Message
Send

15:34
Messages
Dog
Edit
I NEED A HOLIDAY
Yeah. Being a dog must be tiring
IT IS. Where's a good place for a holiday?
Spain is nice and warm
Sounds good
Shall we go to Spain?
WHOA there sparky. 'WE'?
Text Message
Send

16:23
Messages
Dog
Edit
OMFG. I JUST MADE UP THE BEST DOG JOKE EVER
So modest
What do you call a dog who directs action movies?
JOHN WOOF
LIKE JOHN WOO
BUT WOOF
JOHN WOOF
I'm crying
Text Message
Send

16:27
Messages
Dog
Edit
Where are you?
FUCK OFF. YOU HIT ME IN THE FACE WITH A TENNIS BALL
YOU WERE SUPPOSED TO CATCH IT
I WAS LOOKING AT A SNAIL
You need to FOCUS
YOU'RE NOT MY DAD
Don't get weird
Text Message
Send

07:02
Messages
Dog
Edit
TRYING TO MAKE MYSELF A SANDWICH
TOTALLY WRECKED THE KITCHEN
BUT THE IMPORTANT THING IS, I'M HAVING FUN LOL
Yes. That's the important fucking thing
Text Message
Send

11:02
Messages
Dog
Edit
The old woman next door talks to her plants
She's weird
I know. Good job you don't do crazy shit like that
True dat
Text Message
Send

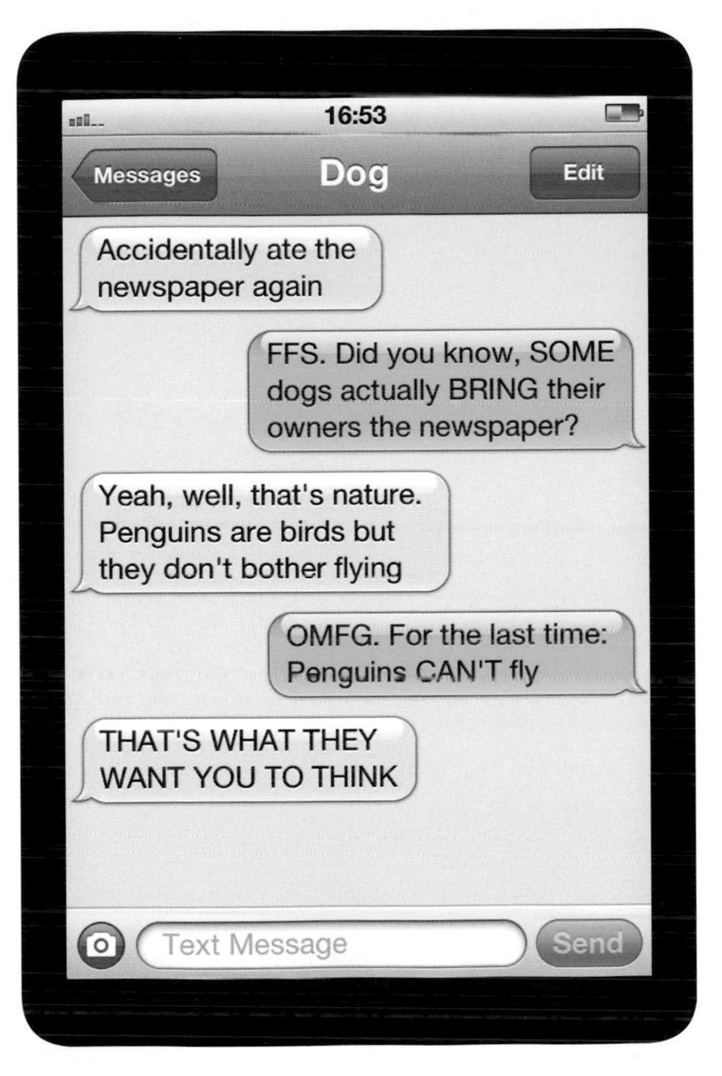
16:53
Messages
Dog
Edit
Accidentally ate the newspaper again
FFS. Did you know, SOME dogs actually BRING their owners the newspaper?
Yeah, well, that's nature. Penguins are birds but they don't bother flying
OMFG. For the last time: Penguins CAN'T fly
THAT'S WHAT THEY WANT YOU TO THINK
Text Message
Send

17:05
Messages
Dog
Edit
My face is wrinkly
You're a BULLDOG
Buy me some moisturiser
You're a BULLDOG
I LOOK OLD
YOU'VE ALWAYS LOOKED OLD
Your face looks like a pile of towels
YOUR FACE LOOKS LIKE A DONKEY'S SCROTUM
Text Message
Send

21:15
Messages
Dog
Edit
The house phone rang
Ok
It rang A LOT
How many times?
1,789 times
WHAT?
NEWSFLASH: I CAN'T FUCKING COUNT
Text Message
Send

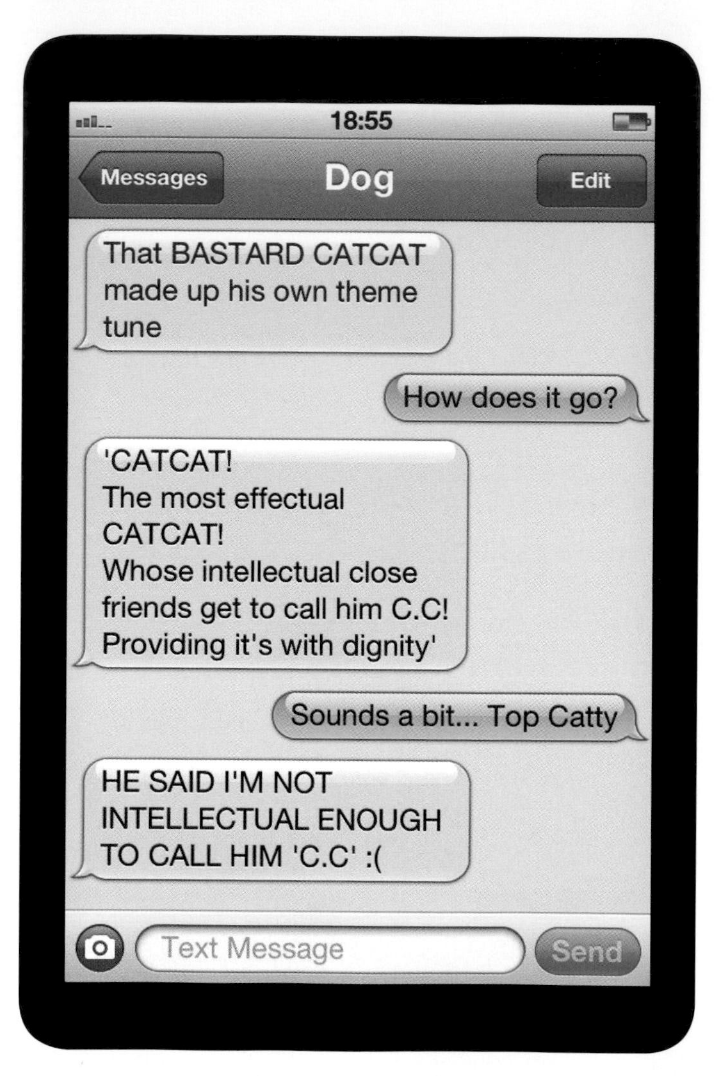
18:55
Messages
Dog
Edit
That BASTARD CATCAT made up his own theme tune
How does it go?
'CATCAT!
The most effectual
CATCAT!
Whose intellectual close
friends get to call him C.C!
Providing it's with dignity'
Sounds a bit... Top Catty
HE SAID I'M NOT INTELLECTUAL ENOUGH TO CALL HIM 'C.C' :(
Text Message
Send

CC

17:19
Messages
Dog
Edit
OMG I FOUND THE STICK!!
How do you feel?
AWFUL. THIS WAS THE WORST GAME I'VE EVER PLAYED
Do you want to play it again?
OMG. I DO!
Text Message
Send

07:55
Messages
Dog
Edit
Did you slip something into my FOOD?
Worming tablets
Are you trying to DRUG ME?
They were worming tablets
I should have seen this coming
WOR-MING TAB-LETS
WHO DO YOU WORK FOR?
Text Message
Send

18:46
Messages
Dog
Edit
WHERE ARE YOU?
On my way home. I'm bringing a mate back
MAN OR WOMAN?
Man
CAN WE TRUST HIM?
Yes
ARE YOU SURE?
YES
I'LL NEED TO SNIFF HIS ASS
Text Message
Send

19:23
Messages
Dog
Edit
WHY DID YOU GIVE ME THIS COMIC?
I thought you might like it
WHY WOULD I LIKE A COMIC ABOUT DOG ABUSE?
What?!
GARFIELD JUST KICKED ODIE OFF A TABLE
ALSO, WHY DOES HE HATE MONDAYS?
THE FAT BASTARD HASN'T EVEN GOT A JOB
Text Message
Send

09:34
Messages
Dog
Edit
I LOVE YOU
Thanks
DO YOU LOVE ME?
Yep
SAY IT
Don't be weird
JUST SAY YOU LOVE ME
I LOVE YOU
ARE WE GAY NOW?
Text Message
Send

22:20
Messages
Dog
Edit
I WANT TO GO FOR A RIDE IN THE CAR
Nope
WHY?
You get carsick in the back seat
SO LET ME DRIVE
Text Message
Send

15:00
Messages
Dog
Edit
Had an AWESOME idea
Ok
Me and you take a bath together...
Nope
WAIT. Then we drop a TOASTER IN THE BATH
That would kill us
You're an idiot. WE'D SWAP BODIES
OMFG. STOP WATCHING SHIT FILMS
Text Message
Send

17:28
Messages
Dog
Edit
ARE YOU A FIGMENT OF MY IMAGINATION?
Yes
Text Message
Send

14:36
Messages
Dog
Edit
How come you've got two names?
I have a first name and a surname
So 'Dog' is my surname?
No
I've decided Dog is my surname
NO
I AM NOW 'MR DOG'
LORD DOG OF BARKINGSHIRE
Text Message
Send

18:36
Messages
Dog
Edit
If I were a human, I would be about 47 years old
How old are you?
29
HOLY SHIT. I'm old enough to be YOUR DAD
YOU'RE GROUNDED LOL
Very funny
ME AND YOUR MUM MADE SWEET LOVE
WTF?
I took it too far
Text Message
Send

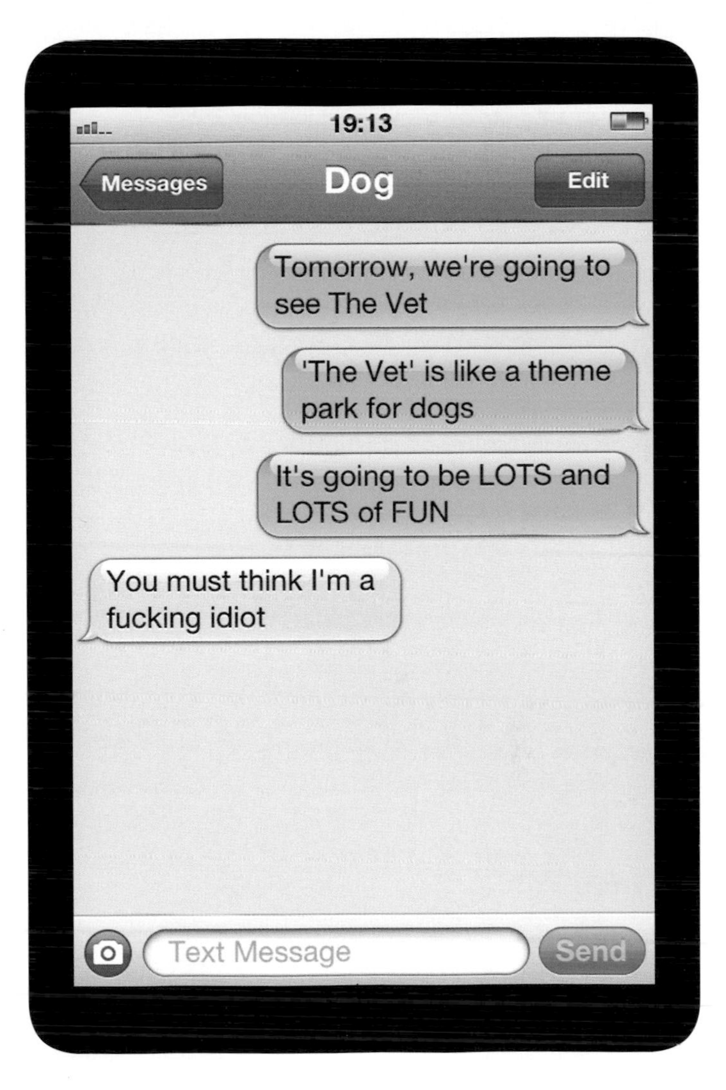
19:13
Messages
Dog
Edit
Tomorrow, we're going to see The Vet
'The Vet' is like a theme park for dogs
It's going to be LOTS and LOTS of FUN
You must think I'm a fucking idiot
Text Message
Send

14:30
Messages
Dog
Edit
WHO'S A GOOD BOY?
Don't talk to me like a dog
WHO'S A GOOD BOY?
ME=HUMAN. YOU=DOG
WHO'S A GOOD BOY?
STOP NOW
WHO'S A GOOD BOY?
I AM. I'M A GOOD BOY
WHO WANTS A BISCUIT?
OMFG STOP MESSING WITH MY HEAD
Text Message
Send

14:52
Messages
Dog
Edit
ARE NUNCHUCKS MADE FROM REAL NUNS?
Yes
Text Message
Send

16:02
Messages
Dog
Edit
Do cosmetic surgeons do tail extensions for dogs?
Yeah. Sure
What kind of tail would look good on me?
Snake, tiger, dragon, lion, monkey. They'd ALL look AWESOME
How much do they cost?
I don't know. I'm talking bollocks
I need new bollocks too
STOP. TEXTING. ME
Text Message
Send

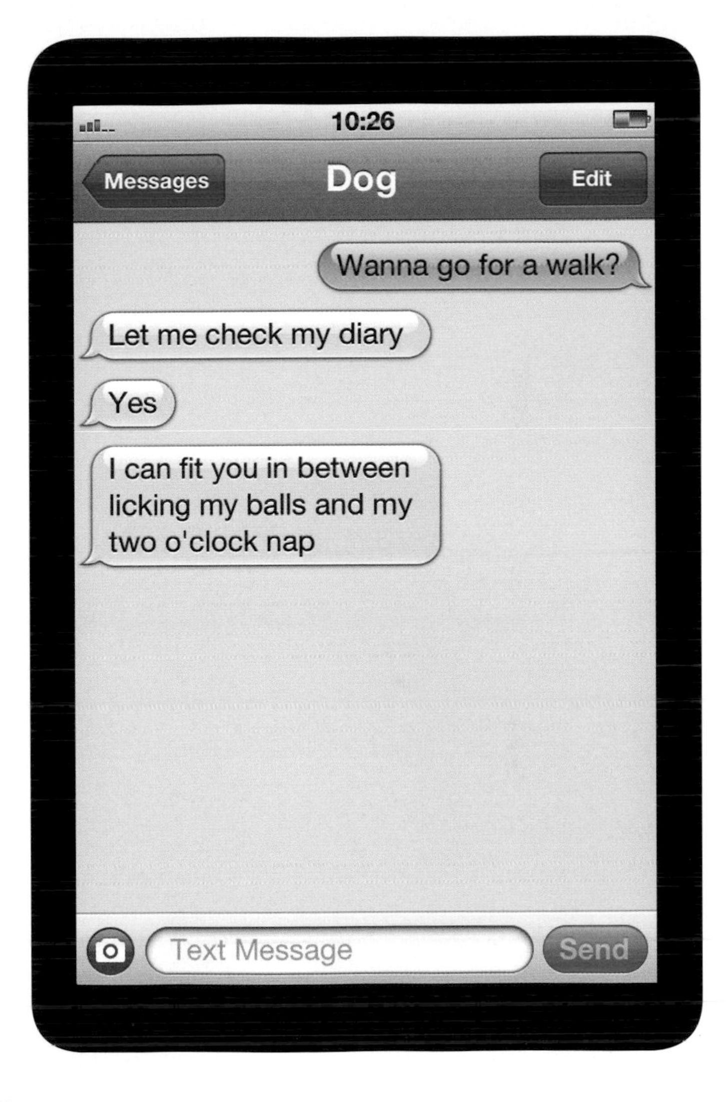
10:26
Messages
Dog
Edit
Wanna go for a walk?
Let me check my diary
Yes
I can fit you in between licking my balls and my two o'clock nap
Text Message
Send

06:45
Messages
Dog
Edit
AM I GAY?
I don't know. Are you attracted to man dogs?
YES
AND LADY DOGS
AND CHAIRS
AND PILLOWS
AND DUCKS
I WANT TO MAKE LOVE TO THE WHOLE WORLD
Right. You're Globalsexual
Text Message
Send

08:27
Messages
Dog
Edit
What will you do with me when I die?
Flush you down the toilet
Is my death a joke to you?
I'm having you stuffed
That would be AWESOME
I'll get a pencil sharpener installed up your bum
If you die first, I'll pull down your trousers and make it look like we were having sex
Well played sir
Text Message
Send

21:28
Messages
Dog
Edit
Just saw this little guy tied up outside a shop
Do you know him?
Yes
I know every dog in the WHOLE WORLD
I sense sarcasm
I sense a DUMBASS
Text Message
Send

13:20
Messages
Dog
Edit
What kind of dog is Yoda?
Yoda isn't a dog
What is he?
I don't know
So he COULD be a dog
HE'S NOT A DOG
OMG. MAYBE I'M A JEDI
Text Message
Send

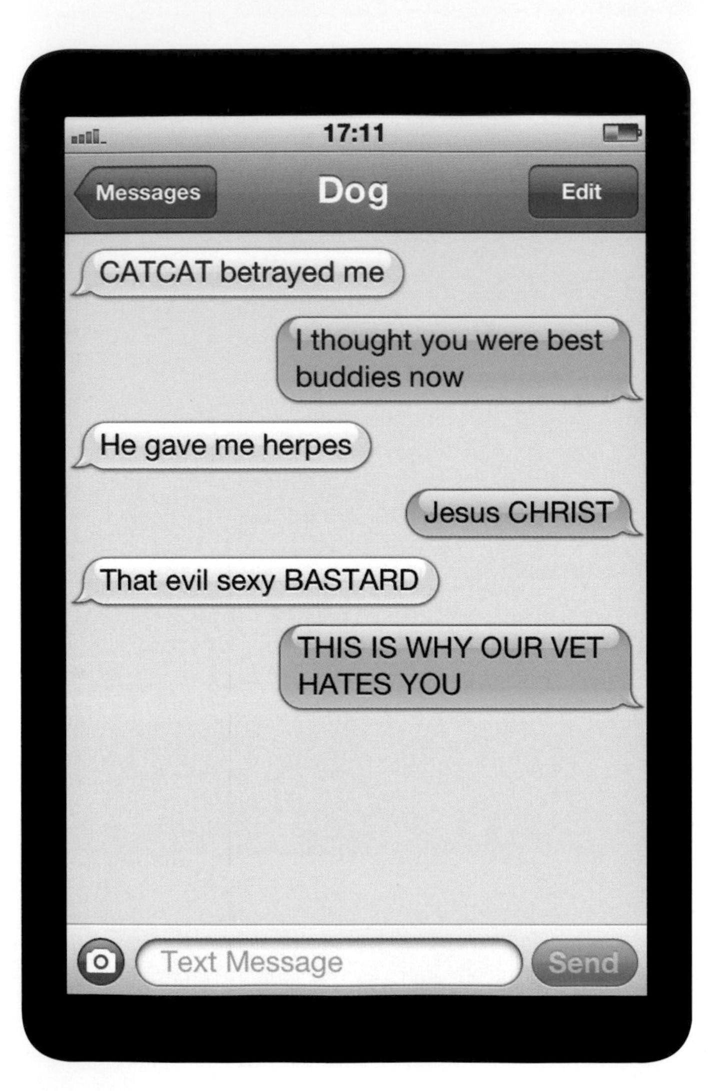
17:11
Messages
Dog
Edit
CATCAT betrayed me
I thought you were best buddies now
He gave me herpes
Jesus CHRIST
That evil sexy BASTARD
THIS IS WHY OUR VET HATES YOU
Text Message
Send

13:27
Messages
Dog
Edit
I have a SIXTH SENSE
Right
I can smell dead people
Everyone can smell dead people
I have a SEVENTH SENSE
Which is?
LASER EYE BLASTERS
That's not really a 'sense'
OMG FUCK OFF DR NEGATIVE. JEEZ
Text Message
Send

21:36
Messages
Dog
Edit
I'm watching a documentary on hurricanes
That's nice. Are you learning anything?
Not really
Has it mentioned Hurricane Katrina?
Were there pants and socks in Hurricane Katrina?
That's the washing machine
Text Message
Send

19:39
Messages
Dog
Edit
What was my mum like?
She seemed alright. I only saw her once
So it was like, a one night stand?
What?
You just 'hit it and quit it'?
I'M NOT YOUR BIOLOGICAL FATHER
Text Message
Send

22:44
Messages
Dog
Edit
We should go on a TALENT show
Hmm. What can YOU do that NO OTHER dog can?
Well?
I'M THINKING
Email me if you come up with anything
I'll Skype you
Whatever
Text Message
Send

14:17
Messages
Dog
Edit
I can hear you talking about me
Unlikely. I'm 25 miles away
My hearing is 400 billion times better than yours
I'll just Google that. 400 billion sounds way too low
I can smell McDonald's
Stop trying to freak me out
McNuggets
CAN YOU SEE ME?
I'm BATDOG
Text Message
Send

17:29
Messages
Dog
Edit
Am I the best dog you've ever had?
You're the ONLY dog I've ever had
I'm squatting over your laptop
BEST. DOG. EVER
In the world?
IN THE UNIVERSE
Text Message
Send

23:40
Messages
Dog
Edit
YOU'VE PUT UP A SIGN SAYING 'BEWARE OF THE DOG'
Yep
WHAT DOES THIS DOG LOOK LIKE?
Like you
Like ME?
EXACTLY like you. It's almost like you're THE SAME DOG
So, he's handsome and DANGEROUS...
Text Message
Send

19:10
Messages
Dog
Edit
I hate this fucking jumper
Leave it on. You look adorable
Why did you buy me this? Do you hate me?
Dogs wear jumpers nowadays
I'm about to go APE SHIT
STAY CALM
TOO LATE
Text Message
Send

09:26
Messages
Dog
Edit
You got a letter
Ok
From the bank, I think
Ok
Tasted important
Text Message
Send

10:13
Messages
Dog
Edit
I'm under the table
I know
What are you eating?
Pasta
Do I like pasta?
No
I probably do
You don't
Really? Because I'm drooling a LOT
And now I feel sick
Text Message
Send

08:24
Messages
Dog
Edit
The Paper Boy is here
He's in cahoots with The Postman
Nobody says 'cahoots' anymore
He's a child delivering papers
Sounds EVIL to me
EVERYTHING SOUNDS 'EVIL' TO YOU
Text Message
Send

22:41
Messages
Dog
Edit
Buy me some pants
What?
I just realised I'm naked. Buy me some pants
I'm not buying you pants
Buy me some pants
I'm not buying you pants
I'm wearing your pants
TAKE OFF MY PANTS
I've wet your pants
You son of a BITCH
Text Message
Send

22:49
Messages
Dog
Edit
Does our house have fire exits?
Er... It has doors and windows
How would we get out if there was a FIRE
I'm not sure
I'll do a test run
DO NOT SET FIRE TO THE HOUSE
FFS, IF THERE'S NO FIRE, HOW WILL I FIND THE FIRE EXITS? DUH
Text Message
Send

08:40
Messages
Dog
Edit
Could you train me to fight?
Like, for dog fights?
Yeah
No
DUDE! I'm a BULLDOG. It's in my BLOOD
Remember when you shit yourself because that hedgehog crawled under the garden gate?
That hedgehog was a drug addict. He had crazy eyes
Text Message
Send

07:32
Messages
Dog
Edit
Did Schrödinger put his dog in a box too?
No
He just fed his dog the poison
Didn't want to take any chances
OMG YOU'RE SO WITTY
Text Message
Send

06:48
Messages
Dog
Edit
LOST MY BONE
THERE WAS A DOG IN THE POND WITH A BIGGER BONE THAN MINE
I OPENED MY MOUTH TO GET HIS BONE AND *MY* BONE FELL IN THE POND
Did you learn something?
YES
THE DOG IN THE POND IS A WANKER
Text Message
Send

23:00
Messages
Dog
Edit
The Dogs Trust commercial says if you sponsor one of their dogs, you'll get letters FROM THE DOG
YEAH, SURE. SOME KIND OF MAGICAL LETTER WRITING DOG
HAHAHAHAHAHAHAHA
HAHAHAHAHAHAHAHA
Text Message
Send

08:00
Messages
Dog
Edit
I was just practising my power slides in the living room, and I had the BEST. IDEA. EVER
What's a power slide?
Two words: PET OLYMPICS
What's a power slide?
It's when I slide round corners really fast. I stopped because I knocked the TV over
OH MY GOD
I know! PET OLYMPICS
Text Message
Send

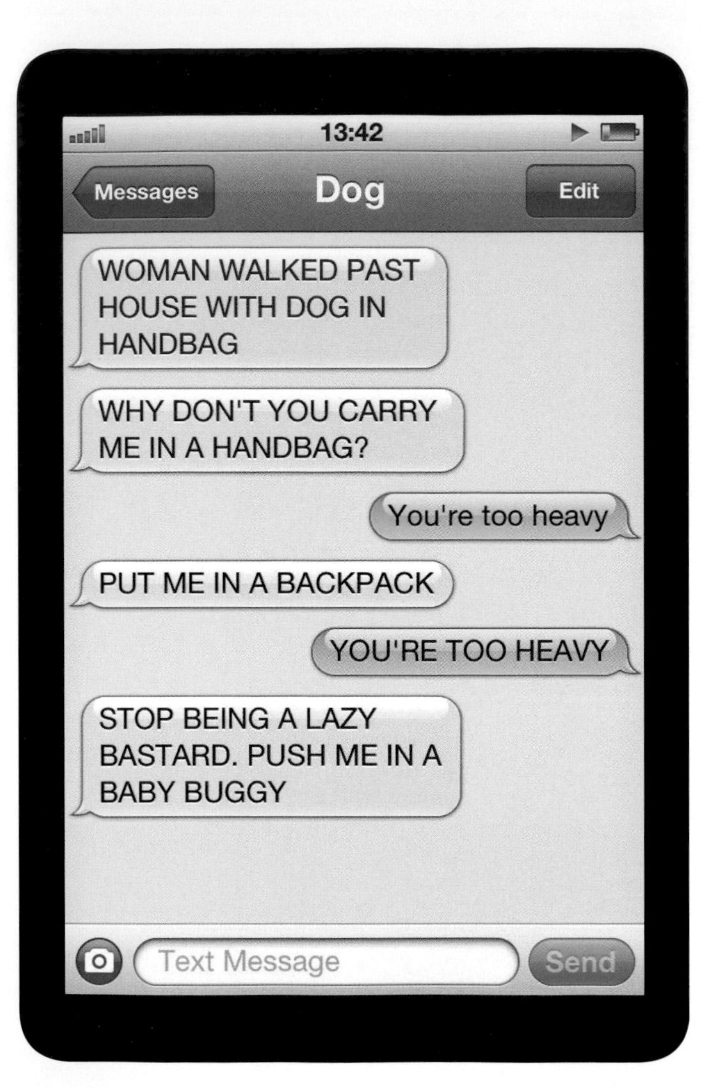
13:42
Messages
Dog
Edit
WOMAN WALKED PAST HOUSE WITH DOG IN HANDBAG
WHY DON'T YOU CARRY ME IN A HANDBAG?
You're too heavy
PUT ME IN A BACKPACK
YOU'RE TOO HEAVY
STOP BEING A LAZY BASTARD. PUSH ME IN A BABY BUGGY
Text Message
Send

23:18
Messages
Dog
Edit
Little kids from next door kicked a football into our garden
I'll throw it back when I get home
Too late. I've burst it
THAT'S HORRIBLE
THAT'S LIFE
Text Message
Send

18:40
Messages
Dog
Edit
Do you think I could be a police dog?
No
I don't think you've got the nerve for it
WTF? My nerves are made of STEEL
Dude, you jump at the sound of your OWN FARTS
THEY SNEAK UP ON ME
Text Message
Send

08:39
Messages
Dog
Edit
How AWESOME would it be if someone made a SITCOM about me?
You mean a SHITCOM
No, SITCOM
SHITCOM
SITCOM
SHIT-COM
YOU'RE SPELLING IT WRONG TWAT-HEAD
Text Message
Send

19:37
Messages
Dog
Edit
REMEMBER THAT SONG, "WHO LET THE DOGS OUT"?
God. Yes
IT WAS ME
Text Message
Send

20:15
Messages
Dog
Edit
Where are you?
Where am I? WHERE ARE YOU?
I'm at home eating Pop Tarts
I'M IN THE PARK
What are you doing there?
WAITING FOR YOU TO BRING BACK THE STICK I THREW TWO HOURS AGO
Oh yeah
Totally couldn't find it
Text Message
Send

07:27
Messages
Dog
Edit
OH MY GOD
What?
JUST WOKE UP. SOMETHING IS HORRIBLY WRONG
EVERYTHING'S UPSIDE DOWN. THE ROOM, THE FURNITURE, MY PHONE
I THINK I'VE HAD A SEIZURE
Are you lying upside down?
Oh shit, yeah. LOL
Text Message
Send

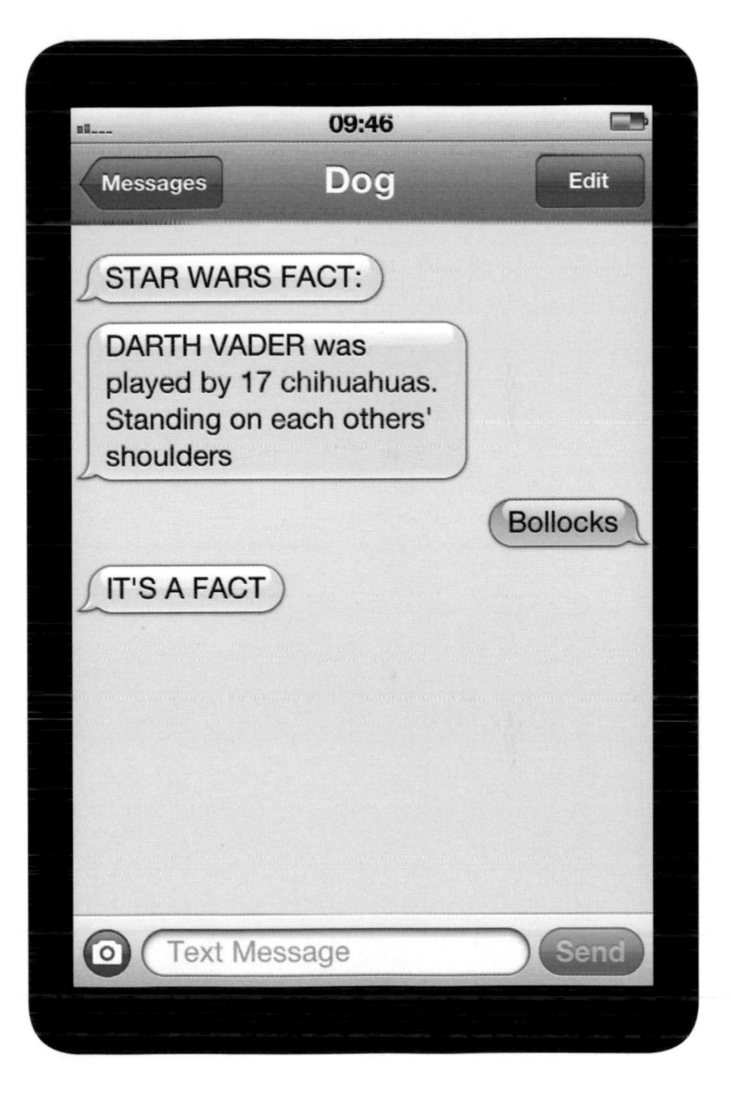
09:46
Messages
Dog
Edit
STAR WARS FACT:
DARTH VADER was played by 17 chihuahuas. Standing on each others' shoulders
Bollocks
IT'S A FACT
Text Message
Send

16:41
Messages
Dog
Edit
OMFG THE PRESENT YOU GAVE ME THIS MORNING IS AWESOME
BEEN PLAYING WITH IT ALL DAY
WHAT DID YOU CALL IT AGAIN?
An old toilet roll
FUNNEST. THING. EVER
Text Message
Send

18:05
Messages
Dog
Edit
I'm in the garden
I know
I can't find that pizza crust you threw out here
THERE WAS NO CRUST. I ONLY PRETENDED TO THROW IT. HAHAHAHA
I'VE LICKED YOUR TOOTHBRUSH EVERY DAY FOR THE PAST 2 WEEKS HAHAHAHA
OMFG
CHECKMATE BONIO BREATH
Text Message
Send

17:42
Messages
Dog
Edit
YOU LEFT THE TV ON
Whoops
I'VE BEEN WATCHING DAYTIME TV FOR NINE HOURS
Jesus
I WANT TO KILL ALL HUMANS
Text Message
Send

13:57
Messages
Dog
Edit
Postman tried to push stuff through the door
That's his JOB
And it's my job to stop him
Who appointed you??
YOU DID. WHEN YOU LET THE SCUM TAKE OVER OUR CITY
OMFG You're insane
I'M BATDOG
Text Message
Send

16:57
Messages
Dog
Edit
Remember when you told me I wasn't allowed to touch the stereo?
Yeah
That was a good call. I just totally fucked it up
You're an asshole
I'M ADMITTING YOU WERE RIGHT. JEEZ. LEARN TO TAKE A COMPLIMENT
Text Message
Send

17:55
Messages
Dog
Edit
Your the best. I love you x
xx (it's 'you're' not 'your')
OH I'M SORRY. DID THE TEXTING DOG MAKE A GRAMMAR MISTAKE?
Don't get hysterical
'WOE IS ME. MY DANCING ELEPHANT HASN'T MASTERED THE TANGO'
Point taken
How's this: YOU'RE going to get head-butted in YOUR testicles
Text Message
Send

21:39
Messages
Dog
Edit
AWESOME MORNING. People said it couldn't be done, but I've been teaching OLD dogs NUDE tricks
NEW tricks
Oh. Crap
Ah, well. They'll be dead soon anyway
Text Message
Send

06:32
Messages
Dog
Edit
WHY HAVE YOU BOUGHT FLEA SHAMPOO?
Er... to get rid of your fleas, genius
YOU CAN'T. I PROMISED PAUL, JOHN, RINGO AND GEORGE THAT THEY COULD STAY
You named your fleas
THEY'RE THE FLEATLES
THEY WERE LIKE 'HELP. WE NEED SOMEBODY'
Text Message
Send

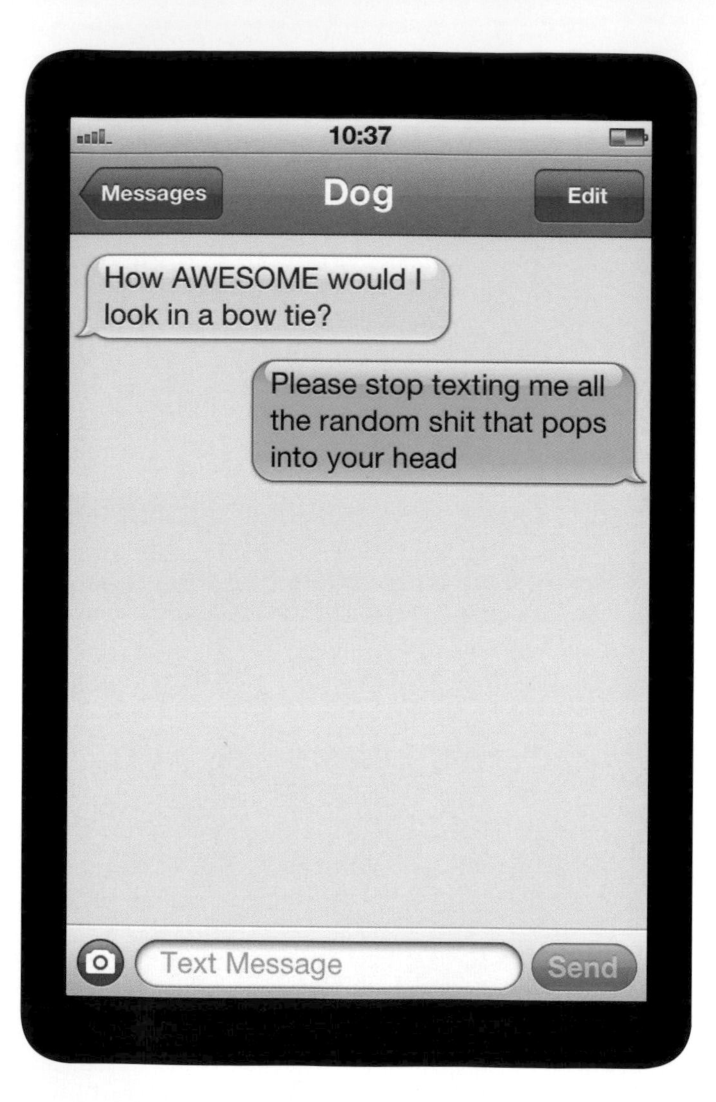
10:37
Messages
Dog
Edit
How AWESOME would I look in a bow tie?
Please stop texting me all the random shit that pops into your head
Text Message
Send

07:40
Messages
Dog
Edit
There's a CAT doing a POO in our garden!
Whose cat is it?
Don't know
What does it look like?
Λ Λ
• •
X
I meant describe it
It's doing another poo
Λ Λ
> <
X
Text Message
Send

21:45
Messages
Dog
Edit
Am I your BEST friend?
Yes :)
Awwwwwww
What a total fucking loser
I love you too x
Text Message
Send

08:43
Messages
Dog
Edit
THIS MORNING THE POSTMAN RUBBED MY BELLY
DID YOU TELL HIM TO DO THAT?
I might have mentioned it
YOU REVEALED MY WEAKNESS TO MY GREATEST ENEMY
HE'S NOT YOUR ENEMY
I'VE BEEN BETRAYED BY MY OWN BUTLER
I'M NOT YOUR BUTLER
Text Message
Send

17:01
Messages
Dog
Edit
Are you coming home yet?
No
How about now?
No
How about now?
No
Now?
NO
Now?
Jesus Christ
Text Message
Send

17:09
Messages
Dog
Edit
Now?
NOT YET
How about now?
NOPE
NOW?
NO
When did you leave the house?
8 MINUTES AGO
Will you be back soon?
Text Message
Send

11:56
Messages
Dog
Edit
WHERE ARE YOU?
At the supermarket
WHEN WILL YOU BE BACK?
Soon
HOW LONG HAVE YOU BEEN GONE? IT FEELS LIKE A LIFETIME
10 minutes
I CAN'T REMEMBER WHAT YOU LOOK LIKE
Text Message
Send

21:47
Messages
Dog
Edit
DID YOU WASH MY BLANKET?
Yes
YOU IDIOT
YOU WASHED ALL THE GOOD STANK OUT OF IT
Text Message
Send

14:47
Messages
Dog
Edit
When I was a puppy, could you tell I was destined for greatness?
Yes. You were delivered to me by a wizard, who told me you would one day SAVE THE WORLD
OH MY GOD. IS THAT TRUE?
It's not is it?
You're mocking me
:)
Dickhead
Text Message
Send

10:58
Messages
Dog
Edit
CHASING TAIL
GET IT. GET THAT TAIL
ALMOST GOT IT
ALMOST GOT IT
ALMOST GOT IT
ALMOST GOT IT
Try changing direction
OMFG TAIL CHANGED DIRECTION TOO
That sneaky BASTARD
Text Message
Send

11:59
Messages
Dog
Edit
TRIED TO CLIMB UP ONTO YOUR DESK
STAY. OFF. THE. DESK
I DIDN'T MAKE IT ASSHOLE. THANKS TO YOUR BOOBY TRAP
Booby trap?
THAT CHAIR HAS WHEELS
I NEARLY ROLLED DOWN THE FREAKIN' STAIRS
Text Message
Send

06:23
Messages
Dog
Edit
Where are you?
I'm on the train. LOOK!
WHO THE HELL IS THAT?
It's a dog. On the train
DID YOU STROKE HIM?
Little bit
DON'T BOTHER COMING HOME
Text Message
Send

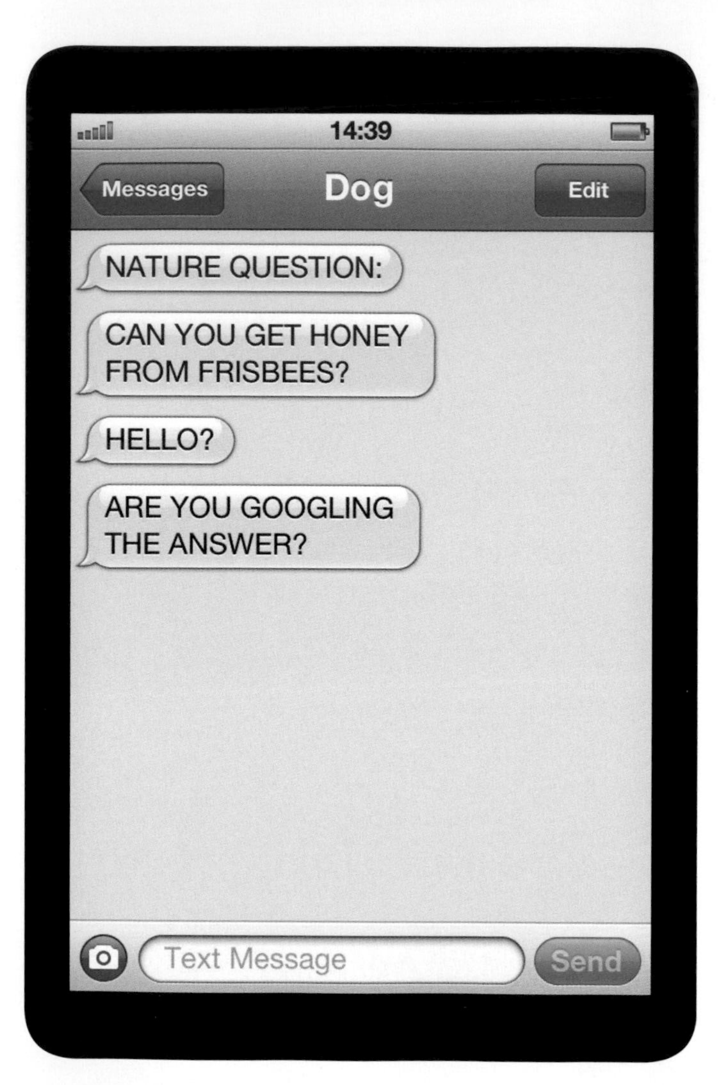
14:39
Messages
Dog
Edit
NATURE QUESTION:
CAN YOU GET HONEY FROM FRISBEES?
HELLO?
ARE YOU GOOGLING THE ANSWER?
Text Message
Send

07:10
Messages
Dog
Edit
What was that?
I FARTED
Nice
HERE COMES ANOTHER ONE...
Text Message
Send

07:53
Messages
Dog
Edit
Got cookie off neighbour
How did you manage that?
Used my SECRET WEAPON
Adorable head tilt?
ADORABLE HEAD TILT
ALL CUTE N' SHIT
Text Message
Send

12:28
Messages
Dog
Edit
Postman's out cold
HOW??
I TOOK HIM DOWN
FFS LEAVE HIM ALONE
I JUMPED OUT OF THE UPSTAIRS WINDOW
OH MY GOD
SHOUTED 'IT'S RAINING BATDOG BITCH'
SAVED THE WORLD
Text Message
Send

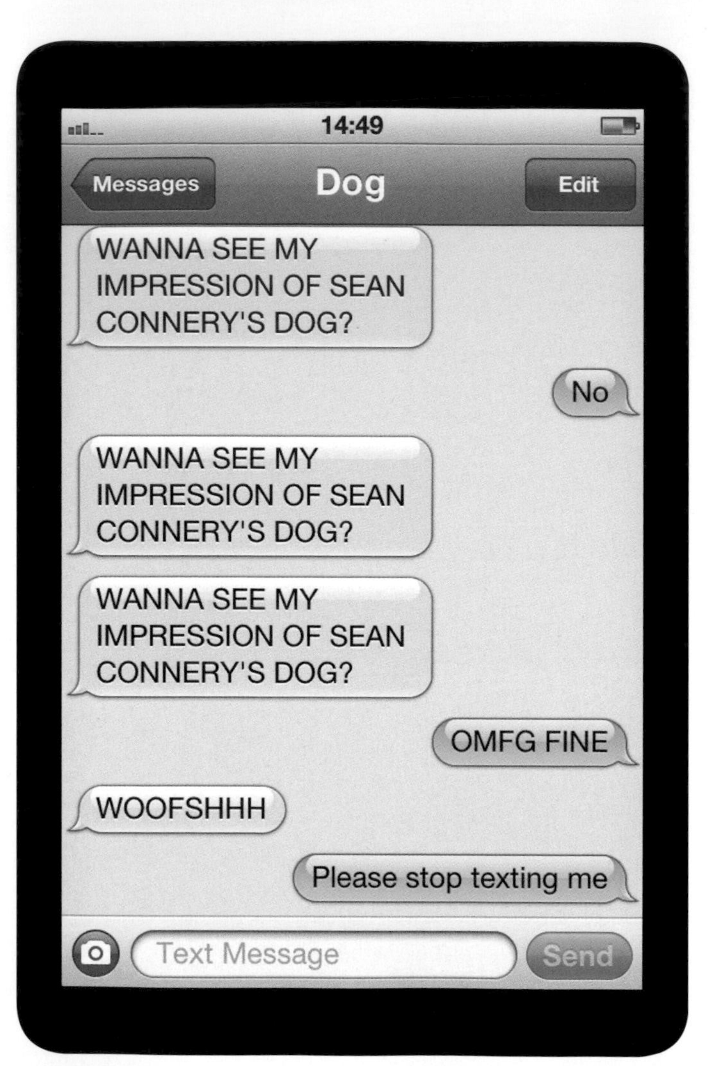
14:49
Messages
Dog
Edit
WANNA SEE MY IMPRESSION OF SEAN CONNERY'S DOG?
No
WANNA SEE MY IMPRESSION OF SEAN CONNERY'S DOG?
WANNA SEE MY IMPRESSION OF SEAN CONNERY'S DOG?
OMFG FINE
WOOFSHHH
Please stop texting me
Text Message
Send

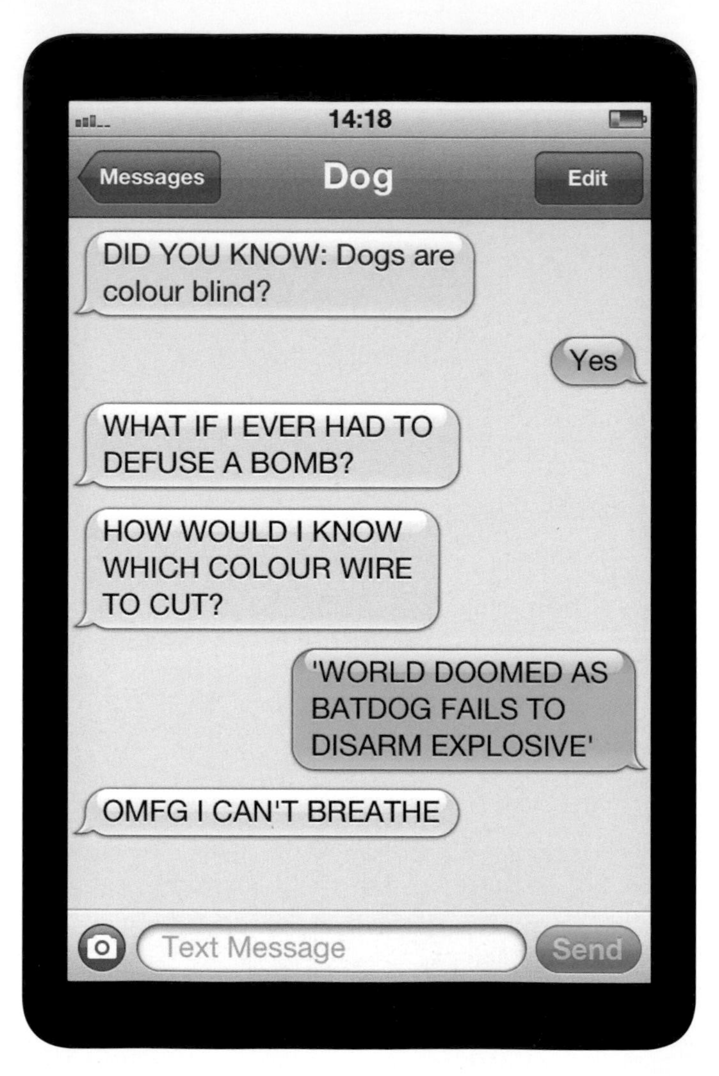
14:18
Messages
Dog
Edit
DID YOU KNOW: Dogs are colour blind?
Yes
WHAT IF I EVER HAD TO DEFUSE A BOMB?
HOW WOULD I KNOW WHICH COLOUR WIRE TO CUT?
'WORLD DOOMED AS BATDOG FAILS TO DISARM EXPLOSIVE'
OMFG I CAN'T BREATHE
Text Message
Send

19:13
Messages
Dog
Edit
Spent morning in garden
Doing what?
Practising slow motion running
What for?
Just in case
Just in case what?
OMFG. JUST IN CASE I EVER DO A DOG FOOD ADVERT. JEEZ
Text Message
Send

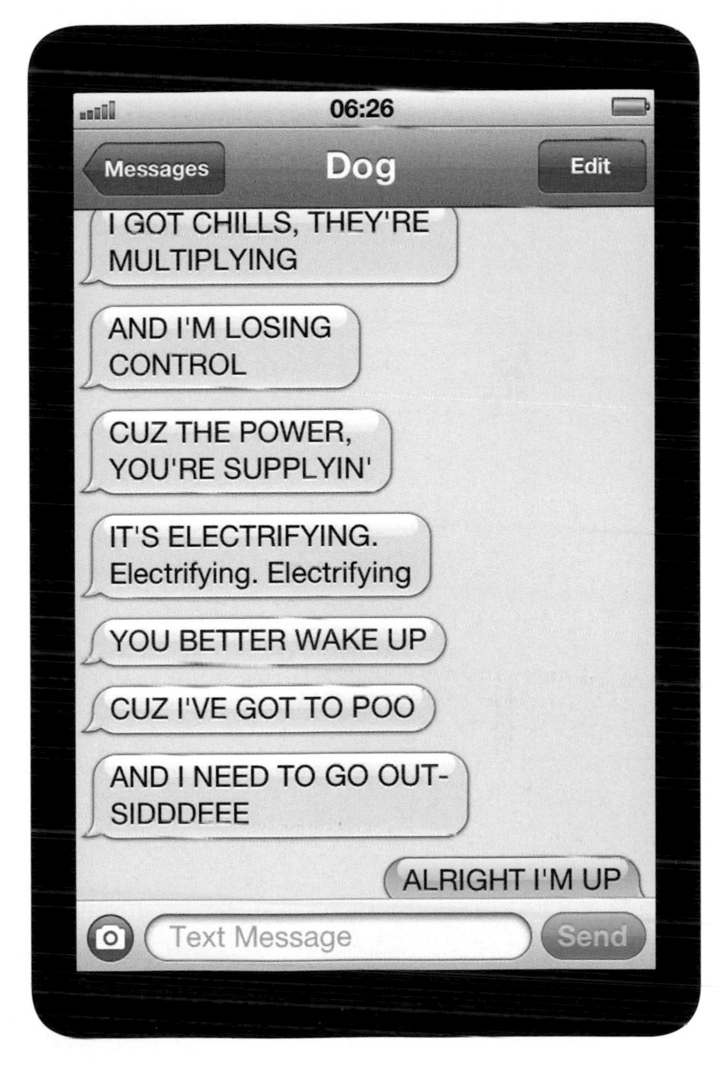
06:26
Messages
Dog
Edit
I GOT CHILLS, THEY'RE MULTIPLYING
AND I'M LOSING CONTROL
CUZ THE POWER, YOU'RE SUPPLYIN'
IT'S ELECTRIFYING. Electrifying. Electrifying
YOU BETTER WAKE UP
CUZ I'VE GOT TO POO
AND I NEED TO GO OUT-SIDDDEEE
ALRIGHT I'M UP
Text Message
Send

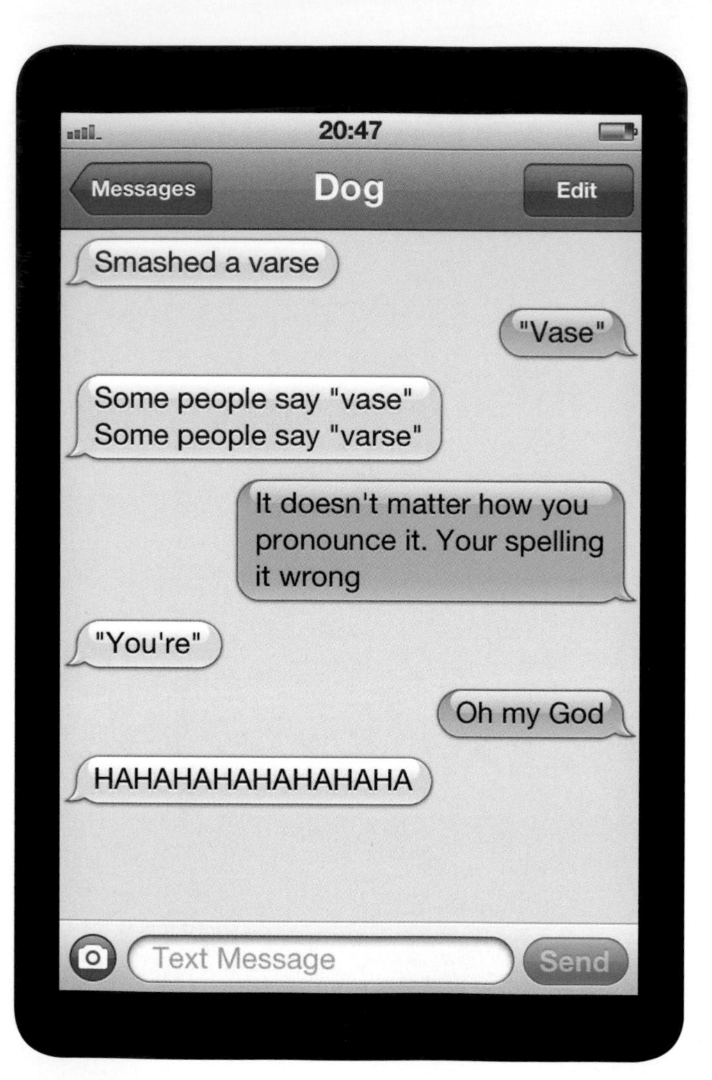
20:47
Messages
Dog
Edit
Smashed a varse
"Vase"
Some people say "vase"
Some people say "varse"
It doesn't matter how you pronounce it. Your spelling it wrong
"You're"
Oh my God
HAHAHAHAHAHAHAHA
Text Message
Send

06:42
Messages
Dog
Edit
CAN'T SLEEP
Try counting sheep
What sheep?
The sheep in your head
BATDOG has no SHEEP in his head
BATDOG's head is full of TIGERS PUNCHING EACH OTHER
Text Message
Send

15:13
Messages
Dog
Edit
PRACTISING STEALTH ATTACK
Don't break anything
BROKE EVERYTHING
QUIETLY
Text Message
Send

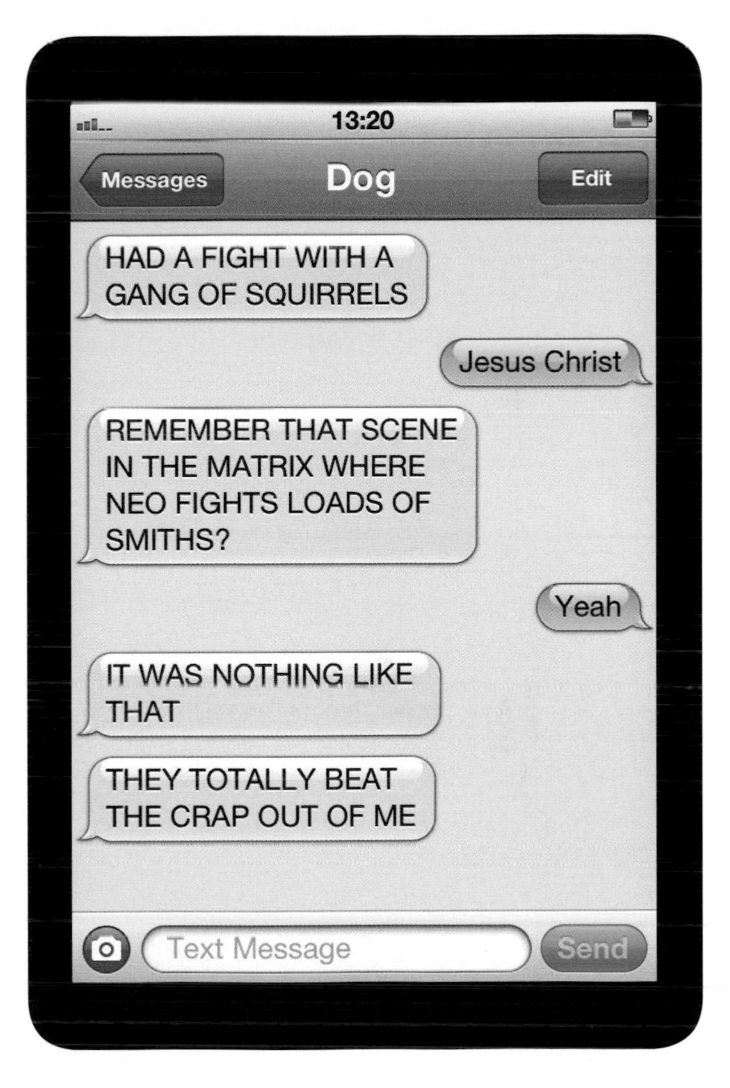
13:20
Messages
Dog
Edit
HAD A FIGHT WITH A GANG OF SQUIRRELS
Jesus Christ
REMEMBER THAT SCENE IN THE MATRIX WHERE NEO FIGHTS LOADS OF SMITHS?
Yeah
IT WAS NOTHING LIKE THAT
THEY TOTALLY BEAT THE CRAP OUT OF ME
Text Message
Send

14:40
Messages
Dog
Edit
HURRY UP
I'm still in the supermarket. I'll untie you soon
I keep going crazy because I think I see you
Then it turns out to be someone else
You know what the problem is? All humans have the SAME KNEES
That's not our fault
OF COURSE IT'S YOUR FAULT. I BET YOU ALL DID IT ON PURPOSE
Text Message
Send

07:00
Messages
Dog
Edit
Awesome morning. Wrapped myself in toilet paper. I'M A MUMMY LOL
STOP WASTING TOILET PAPER
I'm using it to FUEL MY IMAGINATION
You use it to WIPE YOUR ASS
Which of us is "WASTING" toilet paper?
CHECK. MATE.
Text Message
Send

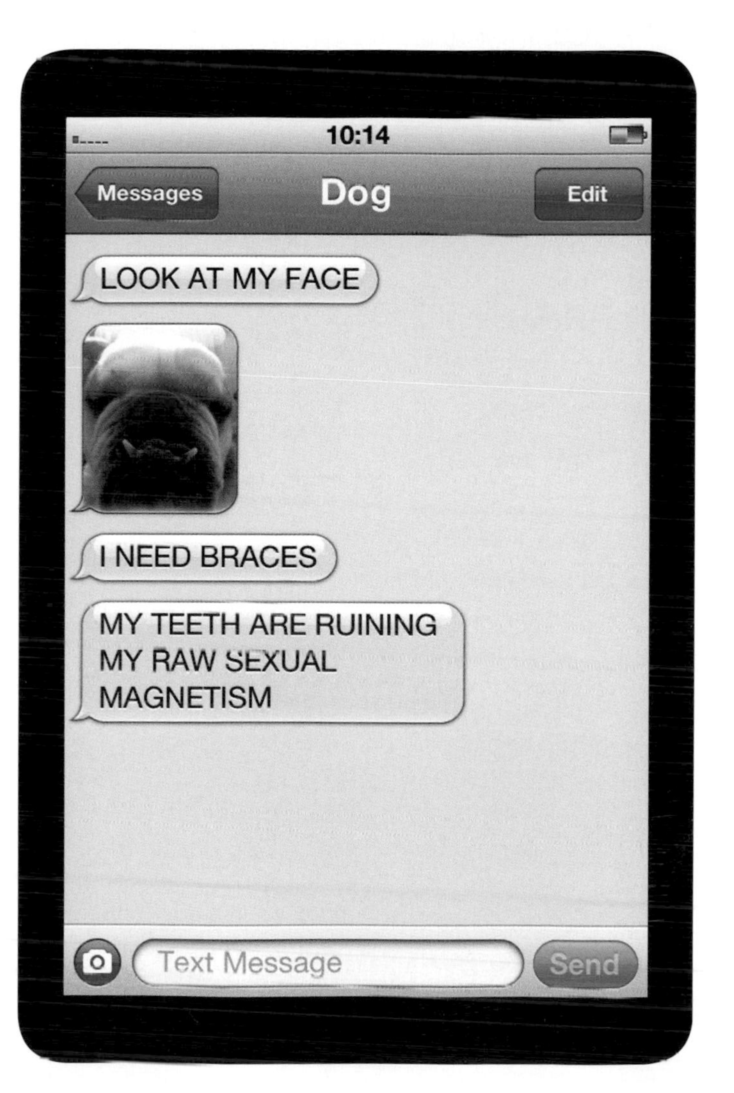
10:14
Messages
Dog
Edit
LOOK AT MY FACE
I NEED BRACES
MY TEETH ARE RUINING MY RAW SEXUAL MAGNETISM
Text Message
Send

17:24
Messages
Dog
Edit
OMG I JUST LICKED A BATTERY
Did you get a shock?
YES. IT WAS HORRIBLE
Did you learn something?
I JUST LICKED IT AGAIN
Apparently not
I JUST LICKED IT AGAIN
Text Message
Send

09:50
Messages
Dog
Edit
CELEBRITY DOG FACT:
PARIS HILTON IS A ROBOT CONTROLLED BY A PUG THAT LIVES IN HER HEAD
Explains a LOT
Text Message
Send

07:58
Messages
Dog
Edit
You left the fridge open
Close it with your nose
I have licked one item of food
What?
I HAVE LICKED ONE ITEM OF FOOD IN THE FRIDGE
BUT WHICH ITEM?
WORST. GAME. EVER.
Text Message
Send

14:05
Messages
Dog
Edit
Did you find the stick?
NO. THIS GAME IS CRAP
Find the stick
I'M COVERED IN MUD
Find the stick
I GOT STUNG BY A BEE
FIND THE STICK
FUCK. THE. STICK.
Text Message
Send

19:22
Messages
Dog
Edit
Stop neglecting me
OH MY GOD. I'm NOT neglecting you
I'll call the RSPB
Jesus, you're an idiot. They protect BIRDS
THEN I'LL TELL THEM YOU'RE FUCKING AN OSTRICH
Text Message
Send

21:50
Messages
Dog
Edit
SCOOBY-DOOBY-DOO
Where are you
WE'VE GOT SOME WORK TO DO NOW
SCOOBY-DOOBY-DOO
Where are you
WE NEED SOME HELP FROM YOU NOW
Twat
Fuck you. That was fun
Text Message
Send

18:23
Messages
Dog
Edit
GOT A TEXT MESSAGE FROM A LAWYER IN INDIA
Ignore it
HE HAS ACCESS TO £5 MILLION IN AN UNUSED BANK ACCOUNT
WANTS TO BRING US IN ON THE DEAL
It's a SCAM
SENT HIM YOUR BANK DETAILS
SON. OF. A. BITCH.
Text Message
Send

16:43
Messages
Dog
Edit
Why are you telling people I've got no nose?
It's a joke
Is that funny? Me losing my sense of smell?
IT'S JUST A JOKE
How about 'My dog's got no legs' 'How does he get around?' 'On a skateboard'
IS THAT FUNNY?
Little bit
You're a monster
Text Message
Send

11:47
Messages
Dog
Edit
Nice chat with the cat from next door
I thought you hated cats
Myth. Dogs love cats
Cats love mice
Chickens love foxes
Badgers love sharks
Everyone hates humans
Oh :(
Don't worry. When the revolution begins, I'll kill you quickly
Text Message
Send

06:34
Messages
Dog
Edit
It's raining here :(
Is it raining where you are?
I'm upstairs
Is it raining there?
We're in the same house. I'm upstairs
IS IT RAINING THERE?
WE'RE IN THE SAME HOUSE
WHY ARE YOU AVOIDING THE QUESTION?
OMFG
Text Message
Send

14:55
Messages
Dog
Edit
Awesome day. I'm doing karate in the kitchen with my NEW SIDEKICK
Sidekick?
Yep. Found him in the garden
Found?
THEY'RE FAST. THEY'RE STRONG. THEY'RE BITCHIN'...
BATDOG & ZOMBIE PIGEON
Get that dead pigeon out of my house
Text Message
Send

16:55
Messages
Dog
Edit
I've hatched a plan
We put up posters of me that say 'MISSING. £500 REWARD'
Right
Then, I HIDE. BUT, I tell YOU where I'm hiding
Ok
THEN, you come and 'FIND' ME
AND WE CLAIM THE REWARD
You're an idiot
Text Message
Send

16:16
Messages
Dog
Edit
Walkies?
Want me to take you for a walk?
I'll take YOU for a walk
Let's get that collar around your neck
Let's get that lead around your wrist
I'M WALKING YOU
ARE YOU?
STOP MESSING WITH MY HEAD ASSHOLE
Text Message
Send

19:26
Messages
Dog
Edit
I hate the way guide dogs get to go in all the shops
That's because they lead blind people
Yeah. But they're like, all up in your face about it
Assholes
Text Message
Send

18:16
Messages
Dog
Edit
What's a 'mistake'?
It's when you accidentally do something wrong
I've never done that
Yeah, ok
You make LOADS of mistakes
I know
What's your BIGGEST one?
Giving a dog a phone
Text Message
Send

09:24
Messages
Dog
Edit
I'm going to grow a moustache
Excellent. Do you know how that works?
DUH. You buy moustache seeds and plant them under your nose
Yep. That's it. Want me to get you some?
Yes please
What kind of moustache would you like?
80s PORN STAR
Text Message
Send

07:27
Messages
Dog
Edit
I'm guarding the house
Good boy
I have a motto. Want to hear it?
Not really
'BURGLARS WATCH OUT/ I'LL KICK YOUR ASS/ LIKE THE BALROG/ YOU SHALL NOT PASS'
What if the burglars have sausages?
I'll help them carry the TV
THANKS GANDALF
Text Message
Send

14:24
Messages
Dog
Edit
SUPER FUN MORNING
Stop texting me at work
GOT HEAD STUCK IN CEREAL BOX
Amazing
SPUN AROUND LIVING ROOM LIKE A FROSTIE SPRINKLER
FFS
FLICKED IT OFF. SMASHED LAMP. THREW UP ON XBOX
IT WAS GRRRRRREAT!
Text Message
Send

10:58
Messages
Dog
Edit
There's a mouse in the kitchen
CATCH IT
WHOA BUCKO
That's not in my job description
Text Message
Send

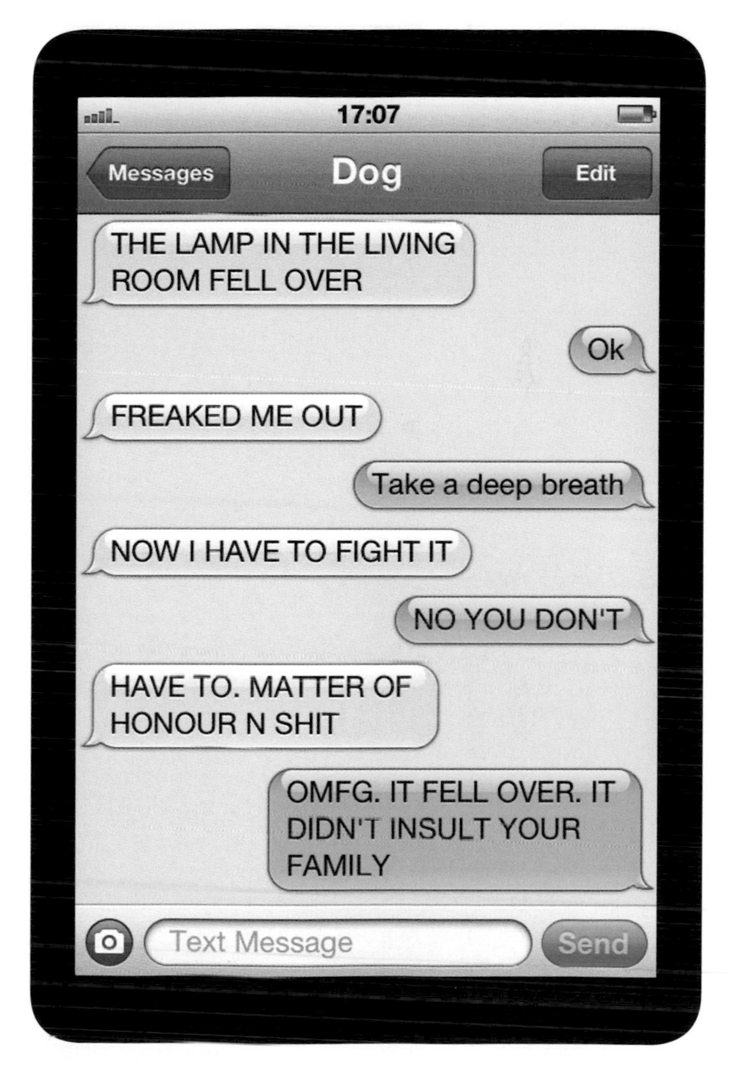
17:07
Messages
Dog
Edit
THE LAMP IN THE LIVING ROOM FELL OVER
Ok
FREAKED ME OUT
Take a deep breath
NOW I HAVE TO FIGHT IT
NO YOU DON'T
HAVE TO. MATTER OF HONOUR N SHIT
OMFG. IT FELL OVER. IT DIDN'T INSULT YOUR FAMILY
Text Message
Send

19:21
Messages
Dog
Edit
My collar doesn't have my name and address on it
I know
What if I get lost. People won't know I live here
Yeah
That would be awful
You evil sack of shit
Text Message
Send

13:53
Messages
Dog
Edit
I just spoke to my friend Ted the Terrier
That's nice
Ted said the vacuum isn't attacking me
Is that right
Ted said YOU'RE attacking me USING the vacuum
Dude, that vacuum HATES you
STOP LYING ASSHOLE
Text Message
Send

08:16
Messages
Dog
Edit
ME VS. LASSIE
Lassie
ME VS. SNOOPY
Snoopy
ME VS. THAT WEIRD DOG FROM DILBERT
The one with glasses?
YEAH
He'd kick your ass
Text Message
Send

14:45
Messages
Dog
Edit
Did you call me? I'm busy
Just got text from neighbour. STOP TWATTING AROUND
I'M NOT. SHE'S LYING
Shall I forward you her text?
YES
'Think your bulldog just ran through my garden with a bath towel wrapped around his head'
OMFG THAT COULD HAVE BEEN ANYBODY
Text Message
Send

19:16
Messages
Dog
Edit
When we meet people, don't say 'This is my dog'
WTF should I say?
You say NOTHING
I'll say 'This is my butler'
Right. What should I call you?
MASTER WOOFINGTON VON BARKSHIRE
Text Message
Send

18:42
Messages
Dog
Edit
I swallowed a spider
Now you have to swallow a bird
What for?
To catch the spider
The spider will dissolve in my stomach acid
Right
Are all humans as stupid as you?
Text Message
Send

15:09
Messages
Dog
Edit
COME AND UNTIE ME
I'm in the bank. I'll be out in a minute
COME AND UNTIE ME IMMEDIATELY
Be PATIENT
THERE IS A CHILD STROKING ME
SHE SAID 'WHO'S A GOOD GIRL?'
Are you a good girl?
I AM BATDOG. THIS IS UNACCEPTABLE
Text Message
Send

23:40
Messages
Dog
Edit
STOP BARKING
I'm doing the TWILIGHT BARK
Like in 101 Dalmatians? That's a REAL thing?
Yep
Who are you talking to?
Ted the Terrier
What did you say?
'YO MOMMA'S SO FAT SHE WEARS A HULA HOOP FOR A COLLAR'
Text Message
Send

23:44
Messages
Dog
Edit
Who would win in a fight...
I hate this game
ME VS. A SHARK
Shark
ME VS. A BEAR
Bear
ME VS. A TIGER
TIGER
ME VS. A T-REX
PICK. SMALLER. ANIMALS. YOU. IDIOT
Text Message
Send

22:57
Messages
Dog
Edit
SUPER FUN DAY
FREE BISCUITS AT THE OLD PEOPLE'S HOME
They don't allow dogs in the old people's home
DISGUISED MYSELF AS AN OLD WOMAN
JESUS CHRIST
Text Message
Send

03:03
Messages
Dog
Edit
I need to go outside
It's 3am
I CAN'T SCHEDULE MY POOS
AT THIS JUNCTURE THERE IS ONLY ONE CHOICE YOU HAVE TO MAKE...
GRASS OR CARPET
I'M UP
Text Message
Send

13:10
Messages
Dog
Edit
What's for dinner?
Take-out for me. Dry dog food for you
Bleurgh
I've laid the table
How?
Fucked one of the legs
That table got LAID bro
Please stay out of the dining room. Forever
Text Message
Send

18:27
Messages
Dog
Edit
Am I anything like my mum?
Your mum was a bitch
TAKE THAT BACK ASSHOLE
Oh wait...
My mum WAS A BITCH
HAHAHAHAHAHAHAHA
HAHAHAHAHAHAHAHA
Dickhead
Text Message
Send

11:18
Messages
Dog
Edit
JUST BEEN BARKING UP THE WRONG TREE
LOL
STFU. SOMETIMES IT ACTUALLY HAPPENS
Text Message
Send

18:45
Messages
Dog
Edit
I WENT BLIND FOR AN HOUR TODAY :(
OMG how? Are you ok?
IT WAS AWFUL. BIT SHAKEN UP
Aw, bud :(What caused it?
TURNS OUT I HAD MY EYES SHUT
You dickhead
I'M OK THOUGH
OF COURSE YOU'RE OK
Text Message
Send

19:27
Messages
Dog
Edit
I've been rubbing my ass on the floor for THREE HOURS
Thanks for the update
You know what the AMAZING thing is?
What
I NEVER GET BORED OF DOING IT
IT'S LIKE MY ASS WAS MADE FOR RUBBING
Text Message
Send

10:16
Messages
Dog
Edit
A Beagle is a DOG
I know. What did you think it was?
Half bee, half eagle
Like, an eagle in a stripey sweater
Are you drunk?
YESSIR
Text Message
Send

10:31
Messages
Dog
Edit
Those are my favourite shoes
Yes
I've taken a photo for you to remember them by
What are you going to do?
WHAT ARE YOU GOING TO DO?
Text Message
Send

10:54
Messages
Dog
Edit
Why don't dogs wear sunglasses?
I don't know. Why don't dogs wear sunglasses?
THAT'S WHAT I JUST ASKED
I thought this was a joke
NO. THIS IS DEADLY FUCKING SERIOUS
Text Message
Send

11:49
Messages
Dog
Edit
I'm going to become a sheepdog
What do you think a sheepdog is?
A dog that's been bitten by a radioactive sheep
Spot on. Let's get you to a farm
Text Message
Send

11:10
Messages
Dog
Edit
WEIRD DREAM
WE SWAPPED HEADS
I LOOKED RIDICULOUS
YOU LOOKED AMAZING
DON'T TRY AND STEAL MY HEAD ASSHOLE
Okey dokey
Text Message
Send

10:46
Messages
Dog
Edit
Need more Bonios
How do you get through them so fast?
I give half to Pam the Poodle. We have a puppy
Say what?
Pam says the boy is mine
YOU'RE IMPOTENT
Oh YEAH
THAT BITCH TOOK HALF MY BONIOS
Text Message
Send

11:23
Messages
Dog
Edit
OH JESUS
I JUST PEED IN ROIDY THE ROTTWEILER'S TERRITORY
Great
IT GETS WORSE
I'M NOT WEARING MY CAPE
Text Message
Send

11:30
Messages
Dog
Edit
CAN'T POO
Don't text me stuff like that
Sorry
DEAR SIR, It appears my back passage is closed for business. Please proceed quickly to the nearest veterinarian and secure me some pills of the laxative variety
ALRIGHT. I GOT IT
GOOD. BECAUSE I CAN'T POO
Text Message
Send

11:46
Messages
Dog
Edit
Why do you have to turn around three times before you lie down?
DOG SECRET
IF I TOLD YOU I'D HAVE TO KILL YOU
LOL
VIOLENTLY
Oh :(
Text Message
Send

08:32
Messages
Dog
Edit
When's 'Take your dog to work day'?
Let me check the calendar
It's the 25th of NEVER
HAHAHAHAHAHA
Isn't that the day you get married?
Bitch
Text Message
Send

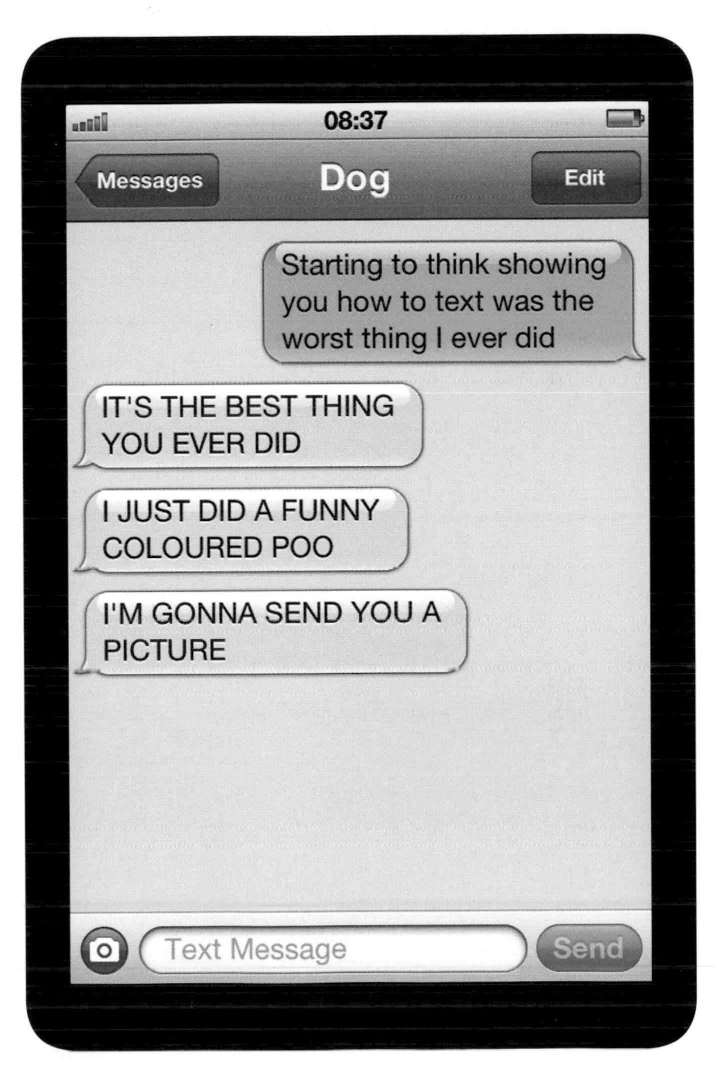
08:37
Messages
Dog
Edit
Starting to think showing you how to text was the worst thing I ever did
IT'S THE BEST THING YOU EVER DID
I JUST DID A FUNNY COLOURED POO
I'M GONNA SEND YOU A PICTURE
Text Message
Send

19:45
Messages
Dog
Edit
WHAT'S ART?
That's a difficult question
Art can be anything
It's a matter of perception
Something that's art to you might not be art to someone else
Do you understand?
NO
THAT SOUNDS LIKE WAFFLY BOLLOCKS
Text Message
Send

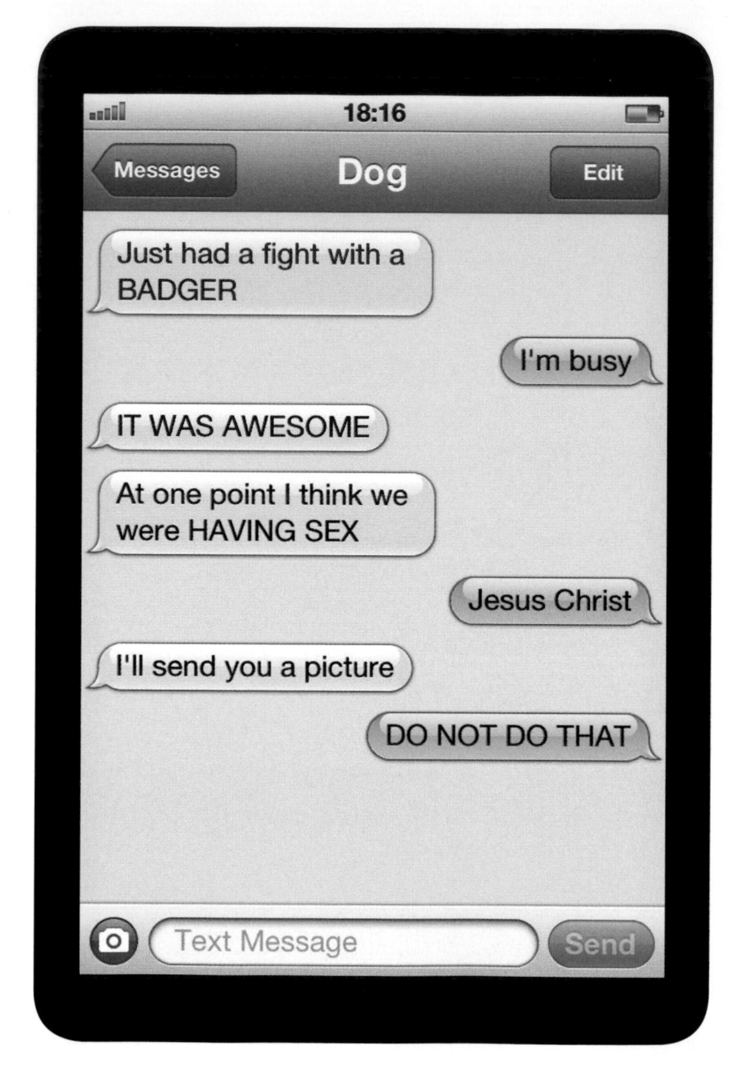
18:16
Messages
Dog
Edit
Just had a fight with a BADGER
I'm busy
IT WAS AWESOME
At one point I think we were HAVING SEX
Jesus Christ
I'll send you a picture
DO NOT DO THAT
Text Message
Send

06:55
Dog
Edit
YOU'RE WRONG
No. You're wrong
YOU COULDN'T BE WRONGER
I can't believe we're disputing this
NEITHER CAN I
PUPPIES ARE WAY CUTER THAN BABIES
YOU'RE WRONG
Text Message
Send

18:16
Messages
Dog
Edit
Y'know the tongue I lick your face with?
Yes
THAT'S THE TONGUE I LICK MY BALLS WITH
Thanks
Text Message
Send

06:57
Messages
Dog
Edit
The old lady next door called me ADORABLE
Let it go
BATDOG IS NOT ADORABLE
BATDOG IS THE CANINE INCARNATION OF FEAR
LET IT GO
I SMACKED HER CAT RIGHT IN FRONT OF HER
Text Message
Send

17:23
Messages
Dog
Edit
Do you think these texts are helping us understand each other better?
Yes
I'm totally awesome
You're a total douche
Good talk
Text Message
Send

DOG & I

OCTOBER JONES was born and raised in Birmingham, England, where, ironically, he spent most of his childhood terrified of dogs. He has recently worked on animation projects for the BBC, as well as doing music videos for UK comedy band The Amateur Transplants.

DOG is the runt of a five-puppy litter born on a farm in Wales. He was the last to be sold, and arrived in Birmingham slighted and grouchy. He spends most of his time napping, snacking, trying to figure out who the second dog in the bedroom mirror is, and, of course, texting.

ACKNOWLEDGEMENTS

Thank you to Kathy and Brent, who made this book possible. Thank you to Sam and Sarah, who always pick me up. Thank you to everyone who supported us online, particularly Andrea Mann at Huffington Post UK. Thank you Gordon and Kristyn.

Dog would like to thank every single popular brand of dog biscuit. He'd like you guys to know that if you want to send him free samples of your products, he'd be fine with that.